You're Stronger Than You Think practically brings us face-to-face with truth, and what happens is what God promises: freedom! Freedom to clear our minds, own our weaknesses, and find His totally sufficient strength. This is a book you don't want to miss!

—**Kay Arthur,** co-CEO of Precept Ministries International

Sometimes when you're in pain, struggle, or difficulty, it's easy to believe either that you have no strengths or that you've lost them. Les's message is so valuable in helping you to find real and dependable sources of strength that you didn't know you had.

—**Dr. Henry Cloud,** coauthor of *Boundaries*

I finished this book thoroughly convinced I never wanted another "near life" experience, and I was motivated and equipped to focus my energies toward a God-honoring, adventurous life.

—**Bill Donahue, PhD,** teacher and bestselling author

This phenomenal masterpiece aligns the mind, heart, and soul in harmony with one another and creates the essence of living life and loving life to the fullest. The completeness of this story-filled resource leaves no guessing when it comes to the validity of life and the value of pure hope, hope that does not disappoint.

—**Thelma Wells, MMin, DD (honorary),** founder of the
    Ready to Win Conferences

YOU'RE STRONGER THAN YOU THINK

THE POWER TO DO WHAT YOU FEEL YOU CAN'T

Dr. Les Parrott

#1 *NEW YORK TIMES* BESTSELLING AUTHOR

Tyndale House Publishers, Inc.
Carol Stream, Illinois

Visit Tyndale online at www.tyndale.com.

Visit Les's website at www.LesandLeslie.com.

TYNDALE and Tyndale's quill logo are registered trademarks of Tyndale House Publishers, Inc.

You're Stronger Than You Think: The Power to Do What You Feel You Can't

Designed by Jacqueline L. Nuñez

Edited by Susan Taylor

Published in association with Yates & Yates (www.yates2.com).

Library of Congress Cataloging-in-Publication Data

Parrott, Les.
   You're stronger than you think : the power to do what you feel you can't / Les Parrott.
   p. cm.
   Includes bibliographical references (p.   ).
   ISBN 978-1-4143-4853-7 (paperback)
   1. Self-realization—Religious aspects—Christianity. 2. Christian life. I. Title.
   BV4598.2.P37 2012
   248.4—dc22   2010018727

Printed in the United States of America

18   17   16   15   14   13   12
 7   6   5   4   3   2   1

To my Strength Group:
Doug Backous
Martin Barrett
David Grieger
Jeff Judy
Jeff Lilley
Brian Muchmore
Steve Pelluer
Jon Sharpe
You make me stronger than you know.

CONTENTS

ACKNOWLEDGMENTS

I want to express my sincere appreciation to everyone who helped me with this project: Kara Leonino, David Lindstedt, Lisa Jackson, Maria Eriksen, Susan Taylor, Jon Farrar, Ron Beers, Erin Gwynne, Jacqueline Nuñez, Gwen Elliott, Timothy Meaney, Bryan Heathman, Michael Boerner, Debbie Kling, Kevin Bell, Brian Muchmore, Geri Bottles, Mark Bottles, Lynda Allen, Brian Allen, Tracy Norlen, Reece Carson, Clint Kelly, Henry Albrecht, Phil Herzog, Dan Price, Rodney Cox, Laila Sharpe, Jon Sharpe, Richard Dahlstrom, Rob Wall, Roger Parrott, Jennifer Gilnett, Troy Snyder, Eric Abel, Loran Lichty, Darin Leonard, Ken Hutcherson, Matt Wimmer, Bill Smead, Jeff Judy, Larry Roberts, Jeff Kemp, Stacy Kemp, Jackie Mosley, Bruce McNicol, Steve Harmon, Barbara Uhlmann, Steve Uhlmann, Jeff McFarlane, Joy Zorn, Carrie Abbott, Mary Myrick, Mike Sullivan, Doug Engberg, Arlys Osborne, Nate Olson, Bobbe Evans, David Wicks, Scott Bolinder, James Smith, George Toles, Janice Lundquist, Leslie Parrott, Kevin Small, Mark Cole, Scott Burbank, Susan Burbank, Mandi Morange, Bill Craig, Ron Keck, Gavin Fysh, Will Raunig, Ed Harowicz, and Sealy Yates. I owe each of you a deep debt of gratitude.

HOW TO GET THE MOST FROM THIS BOOK

Before I move ahead, I want to make you aware of a few supporting resources that you may find helpful on this journey. These resources are not required. They are simply options to help you get the most from your reading. By the way, I hope you might be reading this book as a part of a small group, because some of the following resources were developed especially for this purpose.

THE INVENTORY

To begin with, I encourage you to visit www.StrongerBook.com and take the Online Strength Profile assessment. This questionnaire will take you fewer than ten minutes, and the resulting fifteen-page report will provide a snapshot of your current "strength factors." In other words, it will show you, in specific terms, where you are most likely to find the strength you need. The Online Strength Profile normally retails for $14.95. But as a reader you can use the coupon code STRONGER and receive your profile at the discounted rate of $5.95. You'll want to do this as soon as you can.

THE WORKBOOK

I've developed an optional workbook to accompany this book. It contains exercises and self-tests that relate to each of the six chapters. The workbook has been designed expressly to help you take the content of this book and make it as personally relevant and applicable to you and your life as possible. You can use it on your own or in a group.

When I am weak, then I am strong.

INTRODUCTION
LIFE IS AN ADVENTURE— IF YOU SUMMON THE STRENGTH

May you live all the days of your life.
—Jonathan Swift

It all started—the idea for this book—with an honest conversation between two friends. It went something like this:

"I have to confess something," my friend Bill whispered. We were sitting across the table from each other at a crowded restaurant. I put down my fork and leaned in to listen as Bill continued. "I cried this week while watching a movie trailer on an airplane."

"What?" I asked, half thinking Bill might be joking.

"It was for a kids' movie, but something about it really got to me," he continued.

The way Bill spoke, I could tell he was serious.

"Did anyone see you crying?" I asked, with all the insensitivity I was trained to conceal as a psychologist.

"That's not the point," Bill said, "but, yes, I got a few strange looks."

"What was it?"

"The trailer was for a movie called *Where the Wild Things Are*, and it had this powerful music playing, and then, one by one, these short sentences appeared on the screen. The first one said, 'Inside all of us is hope.' It faded from the screen as the music kept playing, and then the next sentence appeared: 'Inside all of us is fear.' The next sentence made me wince," Bill said. "'Inside all of us is regret.' And then these words, 'Inside all of us is adventure.'"

"Adventure?" I said. "I didn't see that coming."

"Neither did I," said Bill. "But do you know what I feel when I hear those words? I feel like I don't want to miss out on my own life. I don't want to wake up one day and regret that my hopes were never realized. I don't want to play it safe by just waiting on the future. But sometimes I have this fear that keeps me from pursuing my adventure. You know what I mean? Something inside me says maybe I can't handle the adventure or maybe the adventure is too big a risk. Maybe I'm not strong enough."

> Because of the routines we follow, we often forget that life is an ongoing adventure.
>
> MAYA ANGELOU

"No, I get it," I told Bill. "I *do* know that feeling. It's like you have this perpetual hope that someday your *real* life will begin, but you start to think that maybe that's a false hope. You're slogging through the stress and pressures of today while you hold that hope in front of you."

"That's it! And you eventually realize that you've deluded yourself with a false hope because you're feeling that you're going to miss out on your great journey."

"And that's when regret sneaks up on you?"

"Regret, or maybe just the feeling of being inadequate . . . or powerless," Bill said. "Maybe it's just fear. Whatever it is, it keeps you from stepping out of your comfort zone to do what you feel you can't." Bill scanned the restaurant for a moment. "I bet nearly everybody in here, if they thought about it, would feel the same way. We're all so pessimistic. Everybody sees the glass as half empty."

"Not really," I said. "Almost all of the people in here, if you asked them, would tell you they are optimists."

"How can you be so sure?" Bill asked.

IS THE GLASS REALLY HALF FULL?

As it turned out, I had recently done some research on this very issue and had discovered a massive study on the subject. It shows that the vast majority of us—all over the world—see the proverbial glass as half full. At the annual meeting of the Association for Psychological Science in San Francisco, researchers reported on a poll that included 140 countries, representing 95 percent of the world's population. It revealed that 89 percent of us expect the next five years to be as good as or better than our current lives.[1]

So how is it that we succumb to the feeling that we "can't" when we believe our future holds real promise? How can there be such a disconnect between what we say and what we feel? It doesn't make much sense—until you realize that while we may have confidence in the future, we don't always have confidence in our ability to make it through the present. We may see a bolder, brighter tomorrow, but when

> Most people don't aim too high and miss. They aim too low and hit.
>
> BOB MOAWAD

we look at where we are today, our strength fades. We give up before we even start pursuing that brighter future, yet we keep holding out hope that "someday" our lives will be different.

In the meantime, a vague feeling of discontent begins to seep into our souls while we're not looking. Then something like a trailer for a children's movie reminds us that if we are not intentional, our lives will become encumbered with regrets, not so much about what we did but about what we didn't do. If we are not intentional, we become people who "wish we had" instead of those who are "glad we did."

All of this raises the question of how we humans can balance the optimism we hold for the future with the uneasiness we hold in the present. Or, simply put, If the glass is really half full, why do I feel so empty?

WAITING FOR YOUR LIFE TO START . . . SOMEDAY

How content are you with your life right now? Chances are, if you are like most people, you feel you're doing okay, but you're going to be more content, more deeply satisfied with who you are as a person and with the life you are leading somewhere down the road. You're likely feeling a bit unsettled, maybe even restless. Is that right?

Maybe you've heard this little lyric. It makes such a simple but profound point:

> *Each morning he stacked up the letters he'd write*
> > *Tomorrow.*
> *And think of the folks he would fill with delight*
> > *Tomorrow.*
> *It was too bad, indeed, he was busy today,*
> *And hadn't a minute to stop on his way;*
> *More time he would have to give others he'd say*
> > *Tomorrow.*
>
> *The greatest of workers this man would have been*
> > *Tomorrow.*
> *The world would have known him, had he ever seen*
> > *Tomorrow.*

YOU'RE STRONGER THAN YOU THINK

But the fact is he died and he faded from view,
And all that he left here when living was through
Was a mountain of things he intended to do
  Tomorrow.[2]

Do you ever fear ending up like the man in the poem, who died while waiting for the future? Do you ever feel as if you're waiting for your life—real life—to begin? Do you ever feel as if the pressures and fatigue of your daily routine are keeping you stuck, while you continue to hold out hope that the adventure of your life will start—someday?

Maybe the adventure of your life has been put on hold because of something beyond your control. Maybe you've been hit by a curveball, and you're just trying to survive the pain or hardship. Life on hold.

Down deep you know there is more to this life than merely surviving it. You know your future holds promise. And yet the uncertainty and powerlessness you sometimes feel cause you to question your ability to rise above your current circumstances and keep you from doing what you need to do.

There has to be a better way, right? There is. And I'm going to show

> We examine each day before us with barely a glance and say, "No, this isn't one I've been looking for," and wait in a bored sort of way for the next, when we are convinced, our lives will start for real.
>
> TOM HENNEN

it to you. With a counterintuitive approach, I'm going to help you plug into the ultimate power source. I'm not going to tell you to think more positively. You've heard that message before. No, this book is going to show you where to look—right now—for the strength you didn't know you had.

EVERYONE NEEDS MORE STRENGTH

Two human experiences keep us from living the lives we long for. The first experience is the result of a hope deferred—a choice we made out of fear. The second is the result of a hope dashed—a circumstance that was thrust upon us. Let's take a look at each.

Deferred Hope

Life's true adventure begins only when we summon the strength to do what we are afraid of. This can be anything: starting a new career, writing a book, going back to school, or pursuing a relationship. It can be anything that takes us to a place where our unfulfilled dreams are found. In fact, the adventure of living begins when we leap over the great abyss of whatever is holding us back. Most of us tiptoe to the edge of the chasm and catch a glimpse of what's possible on the other side. We may even get excited about what we see—until we look over the edge at what lies below and decide to back away. What keeps us from taking that leap? Fear that we might not make it, right? We see the leap as too great, at least for right now. We believe that we may fall short and the consequences could be dreadful. But we don't give up on the idea. We decide that we'll come back to it, *someday*. We'll take some time and maybe think of how we might build a bridge over the abyss. Or we might wait for better leaping conditions. *And who knows*, we think, *if we wait awhile, the distance may get shorter.*

Whatever our rationale, we put off taking the big leap. We bide our time with the routine of a life that we hope will eventually take us across the chasm. One day stacks on another, and as time passes, we think about the great abyss in our quieter moments. We wonder if we should take the leap soon. But the busyness of our days once again pulls us back from the edge, and we perpetually postpone the leap. Why? Because we are afraid we do not have the strength to make it.

Dashed Hope

Life's great adventure is sometimes foiled by circumstances beyond our control. We don't necessarily lack the strength and courage to leap over the abyss, but we are grappling with a roadblock that puts an end to the journey we were pursuing. We now carry a burden that is sapping us of strength. An obstacle of some kind has thrown us for a loop, and we're suffering from its effects.

No matter how blessed your life may be, if you live on this planet long enough, you will eventually come face-to-face with a sobering season of unexpected pain or hardship. "Not to have felt pain," says an old Jewish proverb, "is not to have been human." A major jolt is inevitable. It may be a job loss, a physical illness, a divorce, an addiction, a relational betrayal, grief, a natural disaster, or any number of other issues that cause emotional suffering. Of course, what causes heart-wrenching pain for some people may barely faze others. But you can count on this: Nobody—not a single soul—is immune to pain.

> Some people spend their entire lives indefinitely preparing to live.
>
> ABRAHAM MASLOW

Albert Einstein said, "Either we suffer in health or we suffer in soul." Some suffer more, and some less, but *all* suffer. We may express our anguish in different ways, but each one of us knows the sting of hardship and heartache, disease and disaster, trials and troubles. And each of us knows that it is in these times, when our dreams have been dashed, that we need the strength we didn't know we had.

FINDING STRENGTH WHERE YOU DIDN'T KNOW TO LOOK

Remember the egg on the cover of this book? It's just a matter of time until it cracks under the pressure, right? Not necessarily. It's not as weak as you might think. The truth is, eggshells are far stronger than they look because their dome shape is able to withstand great pressure. In fact, in one experiment by the Ontario Science Center in Toronto, staff members recorded an experiment in which one unbroken egg was able to support a person weighing two hundred pounds.[3]

So whether you are facing a dream that's been deferred or a dream that's been dashed, this book is written for you. It will show you where and how to find the strength you're looking for.

I have divided this book into three parts: the power of your mind, the power of your heart, and the power of your soul.[4] These are the internal wells where your strength is most likely to reside.

Part 1: The Power of Your Mind

Few experts would dispute the fact that the beginning of renewed strength starts with how we think. We use our minds to analyze, figure out, and plan. Our minds hold our knowledge and understanding.

We've all heard about the undeniable power of our attitudes. But in this section, I propose a new way of drawing strength from our minds. It has to do with simplicity (chapter 1). It has to do with finding strength by clearing our heads in order to discover what should have been obvious all along. Too often, we make life more complicated than it needs to be, and as a result, we get bogged down and become sluggish and exhausted. This section will show you how to travel light and think more simply and, in turn, find fresh resolve and a new tenacity.

I will also show you how to think with expectancy (chapter 2). "Hope deferred makes the heart sick," says the ancient proverb, "but a dream fulfilled is a tree of life."[5] The difference between deferment and fulfillment is found in how we frame our hopes, our wishes, and our dreams. We can frame them with worry, for example, and they are sure to stagnate. Or we can frame them with eager anticipation, and we've suddenly infused them with strength—an electrifying power to see possibilities more clearly than we ever have before. All of this is found in the way we think. And that's the power of our minds.

> **A good head and a good heart are always a formidable combination.**
>
> NELSON MANDELA

Part 2: The Power of Your Heart

While the cognitive part of us may be a starting place for strength, our hearts hold a wealth of power when we know where to tap it. And that, paradoxically, begins by finding the strength that comes when we own our weakness (chapter 3). We realize this goes against conventional wisdom. It runs against the grain of anyone who is trying to appear powerful. But that's the point. This book is about authentic strength that comes from the inside out, not about building a strong facade. And that's why vulnerability, as we will see, is instrumental in finding the emotional power in our hearts.

The same is true of being known (chapter 4). The strength that is found in our hearts will never be optimized until it is connected to other people. When we get too caught up in the busyness of our lives, we lose the meaningful bonds we share with others and, ultimately, with God. And that's why our strength is so often depleted. The bonds built through healthy connection create a dynamic energy within our hearts. They stir our emotions to conjure up strength.

Part 3: The Power of Your Soul

The ultimate source of strength resides deep within our souls. After I show you how to mine the power of your mind and tap the power of your heart, I will show you how to hit your greatest source of power and strength when we look unabashedly into your spirit. For it is there that a sacred secret resides. What is it?

To empty yourself of your striving for strength (chapter 5). Sure, it sounds incongruent, maybe even absurd. But this deeply spiritual surrender, when done properly, is the only way to find the abiding strength your soul desires.

In chapter 6 you will discover a boldness that will likely surprise you. "Boldness," said German poet Johann Wolfgang von Goethe, "has genius and power and magic in it." It can catch you off guard when you see it emerging from within. Yet it is in your soul that your faith, no matter how feeble, can conjure up courage. It is in your soul that you will discover a power greater than you ever imagined, and it comes through a counterintuitive strategy that taps the ultimate power. It is there that you find a direct line to the strength that only God can give. And it rests within the power of your soul.

The word *strong* comes from the Latin word *stringere*, which means to bind tight. Because of the aspect of binding, it eventually also gave us the English word *string*. In a very real sense, this book is going to show you how to tie a taut string around your mind, your heart, and eventually, your soul—uniting and binding them tightly together—to create a powerful grip of renewed strength that banishes every inclination you might have to say, "I can't." It stiff-arms every urge to quit. It makes no room for excuses. Instead, it provides you with the unfathomable power to hold on to a hope that will not disappoint you.[6] It will make you mentally strong, emotionally strong, and spiritually strong. It will give you strength to stand up to your Goliath, whatever it is, look it straight in the eye, and do what you heretofore felt you couldn't.

> I don't want to get to the end of my life and find that I lived just the length of it. I want to have lived the width of it as well.
>
> DIANE ACKERMAN

YOU'RE STRONGER THAN YOU THINK

MY PROMISE TO YOU

If I were to sit down with you and ask why you picked up this book, what would you say? I'm guessing that within minutes, if you felt safe, you'd tell me about a specific situation—a hurdle or a challenge—that is calling into question your resilience or depleting your strength.

And I would listen. I'd listen carefully and sincerely.

Of course, we can't do that through this book, because it's a one-sided conversation. The closest you and I can come to a dialogue is through my website, www.StrongerBook.com, which provides a way for me to hear from you. And I hope I will. I want to know your story. I want to know your thoughts and hear your questions as you move through the chapters of this book.

Every word has been written with you in mind. I've pored over each sentence because I want to be sure my message is clear. Most of all, I've prayed for you, the reader, that this book will serve as a means to nothing less than a breakthrough for you. I don't know the specifics of your life, of course, but I know enough about human experience to believe the message of this book can serve as a pivot point in your life.

> The world is full of suffering; it is also full of overcoming it.
>
> HELEN KELLER

Here's my pledge: You will find no pat answers or spiritual platitudes in these pages. No sanctimonious sayings or stories of false humility. You won't find the proverbial "three easy steps" or ridiculously simple quick fixes. No philosophical mumbo jumbo or psychobabble.

I've written this book for everyone who needs the strength to face down the obstacles that stand between them and their better selves—their better tomorrows. This book is for you if you sometimes wrestle with feelings of insecurity. It's for you if you sometimes doubt yourself. It's for you if you occasionally feel inadequate in your job or as a parent or a spouse. It's for you if you have a broken heart. It's for you if you are afraid to move outside your comfort zone. It's for you if you feel discouraged or overwhelmed by responsibilities.

My pledge, from the outset, is to be real and to offer uncomplicated truth to those who are standing before an obstacle or are staring across their own abyss and are eager to find the strength to do what they feel they can't. If that describes you, then this book is for you.

LIVING STRONG

Before I jump into the heart of this book, consider this parable: An elderly man, in the final days of his life, is lying in bed alone. He awakens to see a group of people crowded around his bed. Their faces are loving but sad. Confused, the old man smiles weakly and whispers, "You must be my childhood friends, come to say goodbye. I am so grateful."

Moving closer, the tallest figure gently grasps the old man's hand and replies, "Yes, we are your best and oldest friends, but long ago you abandoned us, for we are the unfulfilled promises of your youth. We are the unrealized hopes, dreams, and plans that you once felt deeply in your heart but never pursued. We are the unique talents that you never refined, the special gifts that you never discovered. Old friend, we have come not to comfort you but to die with you."

At the end of our lives, we don't want to end up like this old man. Nobody does. We don't want to see our unfulfilled promises and unrealized dreams gather around to visit us in our final days. We want to live life to the full. We want to find the strength to discover true meaning and fulfillment within our obstacles. And we want to muster the strength to take the dreaded leap across the chasm of our fears. None of us want to merely endure. And none of us want to put life on hold and spend our time in perpetual limbo—indefinitely preparing to live.

Some of you, fearing you don't have what it takes to overcome or succeed, give in to weakness. Others show an unflinching determination to find a way through difficulty and keep moving forward. The difference between you is found in realizing that—if you know where to look—you're stronger than you think.

—Les

PART 1
THE POWER OF YOUR MIND

*As he thinks in his heart,
so is he.*
—The Bible

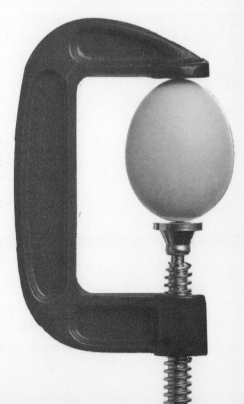

The human brain weighs just three pounds and is composed of mostly water. Yet it has been called the most sophisticated information system on Earth. To say that the human brain is amazing is an understatement.

Consider what your brain is doing right now, while you are reading these words. Your occipital lobes, near the back of your head, are processing how you see this sentence. And the frontal lobes of your cerebral cortex are engaged in thinking through the meaning of these words. They are helping you see how the content might apply to you. Meanwhile, you just blinked because of the motor area of your brain. The cerebellum, in the lower portion of your brain, enables you to hold this book in your hands, as well as do anything else you're doing right now that calls for balance and coordination—like sitting. All the while, your metabolism and hormonal functions, such as the ones that regulate the water and sugar levels in your body, are currently being controlled by your pituitary gland, deep inside your brain. And if you are sitting outside on a park bench on a cold, wintry day while you're reading this, your hypothalamus is responsible for warning you to go inside by causing you to shiver. You'll remember what you're reading in this paragraph because of your hippocampus, whose job it is to translate short-term memory into long-term memory. It also enables you to remember that the point of this elaborate example is to underscore how complex and marvelous your brain is.

We don't have to read the *Journal of Neuroscience* to realize that the human brain is remarkable. We've all heard how even the most advanced computers can't hold a candle to the human brain. In fact, a computer comparable to the human brain would need to be able to perform more than 38 thousand trillion operations per second.[1] Our brains make computers look like Tinkertoy sets. We can, for example, recognize a friend right after she's had her hair cut. When we hear "Shall I compare thee to a summer's day?" we don't expect a weather report. When someone asks us if we know Bob Thompson, who plays the trumpet in the school band and lives on Maple Street, we answer yes, but we know that his name is actually Bill, not Bob, and that he plays the trombone and moved away six months ago. We can recognize something as a chair, whether it's a beanbag, a Chippendale side chair, or a throne. We cn undrstin wrds efen wen theh ar missspld. Or fill in the blanks when lttrs are missing.

As you are reading the words on this page, your brain is sending electrical impulses through a network of brain cells so small that thousands of them could fit into the period at the end of this sentence. We take this kind of mental work for granted, but computers can't even come close. The brain simply runs too efficiently for it to be a fair competition.

As I said, to say the human brain is amazing is simply an understatement. Complete understanding of the brain will be a long time coming. But truth be told, the physical human brain is child's play compared to the intangible human mind. "The mind is its own place," said English poet John Milton, "and in it self, can make a Heav'n of Hell, a Hell of Heav'n."[2] Scientists have pretty well mapped out the terrain of the brain, but they are far from understanding the complexities of the mind. After all, it's not possible to x-ray the mind. It's beyond physical location. French philosopher René Descartes declared that the mind, while it might live in the brain, was a nonmaterial thing, entirely separate from the physical tissues found inside the head. Furthermore, said Descartes, in one of history's most memorable sound bites, "I think, therefore I am." His point was that consciousness is the only sure evidence that we actually exist. Pardon the pun, but the mind is pretty heady. It leaves scientists and philosophers alike with much to ponder.

What scientists *do* know about the mind is that it is an intensely private part of each individual. Nobody but the owner has access to its intuitive and rational parts. No one else can know your mind unless you choose to share it. Your mind holds your sense of self. It is synonymous with your thoughts. Thus, you "make up your mind," you "change your mind," or you are sometimes "of two minds." In fact, it's sometimes said that the mind is what your brain does. Your mind, in a word, thinks.

THINKING SIMPLY AND EXPECTANTLY

In the two chapters in part 1, I will show you how to tap the power of your mind—how to think with strength.

Chapter 1, "Think Simply," reveals the "sacred gift" offered to those who learn how to clear their heads. We all long for that gift, when we think about it, but we too often neglect it. By the way, thinking simply is not simple thinking. To say it another way, thinking simply is not the same as being simpleminded. And it's certainly not the same as being a simpleton. A simpleton is a fool, someone who lacks wisdom and knowledge: "A prudent person foresees danger and takes precautions. The simpleton goes blindly on and suffers the consequences."[3] The simpleton uses poor judgment—the very thing *simple* thinking guards against. In fact, as you will see in chapter 1, thinking simply is the only sure path to wisdom.

Chapter 2, "Think Expectantly," takes an even more powerful step toward mining the power of your mind. Hundreds of studies in this area have stunned even the researchers. In one classic example, blindfolded subjects can be told that a hot knife will be applied to their skin for only a second. In reality, "a cold knife touches the skin very lightly and produces a burn blister. The heat, obviously, is furnished by the mind."[4] This chapter will show you how to harness your expectations and gain more meaningful results. In fact, it will show you how thinking expectantly can tap into the ultimate meaning of life with a hope that will not disappoint.

YOUR MIND IS STRONGER THAN YOU KNOW

Before we jump into the first two chapters, I want to remind you of a story you have surely encountered before:

A fierce and powerful lion once ruled the forest. His great size and regal demeanor made him unapproachable, and he was feared by all the other creatures of his kingdom. From a safe distance they watched his mighty, muscular frame move along the forest paths, and his reputed bravery became legendary.

One day, he came upon a child who had never heard of him and his fearful power. The child approached him innocently, and lo and behold, the lion shrank back and cowered behind a tree, shaking with fear.

"What's wrong?" the child asked kindly.

The lion could scarcely speak because he was trembling so. "I—I'm . . . afraid."

"But you're a lion. I thought lions were strong and brave."

"Not me," the lion answered miserably. "Everyone thinks I'm powerful and fearless, but everything scares me. I'm not strong at all."

"You poor thing. I'm on my way to see a very wise man who may be able to help you. I've heard he can do amazing things."

"Do you really think he could make me strong and brave?"

"Let's go and see."

So off went the lion and the child to find the wise man who could make the lion strong. When they found him, the wise man looked into the lion's eyes and said, "You've been strong and brave all along. But here's a badge to wear that will remind you that the strength you seek is already in you."

By now, you have probably realized that this scenario is from the film *The Wizard of Oz*, based on the book *The Wonderful Wizard of Oz*, by L. Frank Baum. You may also recall what the Wizard offered Dorothy's three companions: He gave the Tin Woodman a ticking heart, and to the Scarecrow he gave a diploma, which made him "officially" smart. As for the Cowardly Lion, he received only a tangible reminder of what was already inside him, ready to be appropriated. The Wizard might have said to the Cowardly Lion, "You're stronger than you think."

1

THINK SIMPLY
THERE'S STRENGTH IN CLEARING YOUR HEAD

The intuitive mind is a sacred gift and the rational mind is a faithful servant. We have created a society that honors the servant and has forgotten the gift.
—ALBERT EINSTEIN

Josh Waitzkin caught his first glimpses of chess sets when he was just six years old. One day, he was walking with his mother through a park in Manhattan, heading for the monkey bars. When Josh spotted an elderly man sitting at one of the park's chess tables, he impulsively ran over to the gentleman and asked, "Wanna play?"

Josh's mom apologized and explained that Josh didn't know how to play chess. But the man welcomed little Josh to the table and began to set up the pieces. That's when something strange happened. "As we moved the pieces," Josh recounted as an adult, "I felt like I had done this before." A crowd soon gathered around the board, as the young boy seemed to know instinctually what to do. Josh's mother was confused and a little concerned about her son. Without warning, he seemed to move into another dimension, where the complexities of chess came easily.

Josh, it turned out, was a prodigy—gifted beyond belief. He returned again and again to the park to play chess with the locals. He was a phenomenon, a natural. The park guys leveraged his raw talent and taught Josh their aggressive, intuitive style of competition. And it paid off.

At age seven, Josh began his classical study of the game with his first formal teacher. From age nine on, he dominated the U.S. scholastic chess scene. He won the National Primary Championship, the National Junior High Championship, and while in the fifth grade, the National Elementary Championship. At the age of eleven, he played a match with World Champion Garry Kasparov in a simultaneous exhibition. At thirteen, Josh earned the title of National Master.[1]

Under the tutelage of a strict and demanding teacher, Josh learned complex formulas and endless combinations of moves. He could outthink nearly any opponent. But somewhere along the line, his thinking became too complex. His head was filled with so many strategies that his brain began locking up.

> **God's providence is on the side of clear heads.**
>
> HENRY WARD BEECHER

The film *Searching for Bobby Fischer* depicts a particularly tense match with another prodigy. The two are playing alone, with cameras making their game visible to parents and trainers in another room.[2] As Josh's teacher watches, Josh struggles with his next, critical move. He sees the pieces on the board, but he can't see what to do next.

"It's there. See it, Josh," his teacher whispers to himself. Suddenly Josh's mind clears, and he sees the board empty of its pieces. He immediately knows his next move, and it's the winning one.

Seeing an *empty* board? How could that help him? As it turns out, Josh's teacher had to show his pupil the most important move he would make in becoming a champion: how to clear his head.

As part of the training process, he literally had to help Josh think more simply. Josh had to unlearn the patterns and formulations he had devised and developed. He had to learn how to think beyond the pieces on the board.

"You're letting the pieces get in your way," his teacher would say. "You've got to clear your mind," he said on one occasion and then swept the pieces off the board with his arm. "Now make your next move."

It was his way of helping Josh uncover his true strength. It's what allowed Josh to recover his giftedness and power as a player. The clutter and complexity of too much information and too much thinking were holding Josh back. It was slowing him down. What Josh needed was to clear his head to regain his strength.

It may sound paradoxical, but it's true. And the same principle applies to all of us. We can make life more complicated than it needs to be. We can cloud our minds with too much thinking, too much analyzing. And when we do, we lose the strength and clarity we need to make the next move.

That's why I dedicate the first chapter of this book to helping you think more simply. I dedicate this chapter to the idea of clearing your head.

ARE YOU THINKING TOO MUCH?

"Life is deep and simple, and what our society gives us is shallow and complicated." These are the words of the renowned Fred Rogers, better known as Mister Rogers, on the children's television program *Mr. Rogers' Neighborhood*. He uttered the words shortly before he passed away. What an insightful sentence. Life *is* deep and simple. And yet we so often make it more complicated than it needs to be—because we think too much.

Just about anything can trigger overthinking: Your boss makes a sarcastic comment; your spouse doesn't call when you expect it; a colleague seems short with you in an e-mail; a friend makes a flippant comment about your weight; you're nervous about a doctor's appointment. The list is endless. You ruminate on these situations, postulating possible explanations for other people's actions, picking apart scenarios, replaying the events in your head, and coming up with alternate endings—basically creating a "thought fog" in your brain.

You may think you're gaining valuable insight by analyzing every detail, but you're not. Overthinking is not your friend. It makes your mind tense, keeps you stuck in your head, and immobilizes your motivations. So the question remains: Are you thinking too much?

> **We are dying from overthinking. We are slowly killing ourselves by thinking about everything. Think. Think. Think.**
>
> ANTHONY HOPKINS

If you're like most people, you probably are. We live in a self-analytical culture. Most of us complicate our existence on occasion because our minds are working overtime. What are we busy thinking about? Take your pick: relationships, health, money, work, the future—the normal stuff. The stuff life is made of. That's why overthinking is so endemic.

Fold together a few of the mental tensions bombarding your brain—say a dozen or more of them in a single week—and you have a surefire recipe for a fuzzy head. What's the result? You literally become weaker. People sometimes joke about how it hurts to think, and there's actually an element of truth to that. Scientists from the University of Illinois have proof that overthinking makes us tired. It has to do with the fact that our brains need glucose to function, and when our thoughts are running in high gear, we use up glucose faster than we do when our brains aren't running at high speed.[3] The result is mental fatigue and exhaustion.

Overthinking really does strain your brain. And that's not all. Overthinking dulls your focus. Your physical energy ebbs. You lose perspective, and little problems can seem to be disasters. You feel overwhelmed or sometimes even out of control. These tensions paralyze your brain and cloud your mind. Worries, obsessions, and concerns overload your thinking, complicate your life, and weaken your efforts to take healthy strides forward.

Imagine this scenario: You're a young mother with a toddler and a baby who's teething. The washing machine quit working yesterday just as you got the first load in, but that's okay because the repairman is coming, and the piles of laundry on the floor will be gone by tonight. You're thinking you'll order carryout for dinner. That will save time and allow you to work on the laundry while the kids nap. *This will work*, you decide. *I just need to be flexible.*

Then the phone rings. It's your husband, who says he really needs you to work some magic on dinner tonight because he's bringing home a client from out of town (the client who made demeaning remarks to you the last time he visited, and you still haven't managed to put that behind you). At this point, your brain is shifting into high gear. *Okay, forget the laundry. I'll push the piles into the bedroom, close the door until tomorrow, and concentrate on dinner. Although it won't matter what I make. Having to play host to that guy again is going to ruin what's left of my day!*

You've no sooner pulled out your recipe file than you hear, "Mommy, something's wrong!" You drop the recipes and arrive in the living room to see the goldfish lying on their sides at the top of the water and your toddler struggling to put the lid back on the Elmer's glue bottle.

Any one of these "irritations" by itself would be just that—an irritation. But all together . . . How focused are you on dinner or the fish or the laundry now? Maybe all you can focus on is putting the kids to sleep as soon as possible and crawling under the covers yourself.

Be honest. Do you ever catch your mind working overtime?

Do you find yourself dwelling on past events and situations and overanalyzing them, replaying them, worrying about how you handled them? If so, you're not alone, and this chapter is going to help you regain the strength and clarity your cluttered mind has been stealing from you. First, we're going to take a closer look at the idea of mind fog.

HOW MIND FOG DEVELOPS

Legendary golfer Chi Chi Rodriguez has long lamented his poor putting ability. "If I could putt, you would've never heard of Arnold Palmer," he has been known to say. But Rodriguez wasn't always a poor putter. Early in his career he was a great putter. What happened?

"I never knew what I did putting," Rodriguez said. "I just knew that there was a hole, there was a ball, there was a putter, I was supposed to knock the ball in the hole. . . . A magazine paid me $50 to figure out what I did putting, and I haven't putted good since."[4]

So what happened to Chi Chi's putting? Overthinking happened. Actually, it happened to his mind, and that's what threw his putting out of whack. We know this because a group of scientists studying the "paralysis of analysis" have shown that thinking too much has an impact on a person's performance. Golfers provide a good example. Too much analysis makes their game worse. Neuroscientist Michael Anderson, of the University of St. Andrews in Scotland, says that the loss of performance in nearly any area is the result of an effect called verbal overshadowing.[5] This occurs when we activate the language centers of our brains and, in a sense, overload them when we need to be accessing other areas of our brains that give us new perspectives.[6]

> Clear thinking requires courage rather than intelligence.
>
> THOMAS S. SZASZ

That's the point of thinking simply. Clearing our minds puts an end to our stuckness. It loosens up our paralysis analysis and relaxes the tension in our heads. *When you clear your head—when you still your rational mind enough to make room for your intuitive mind—you're creating space for wisdom. You're not letting go of rational thoughts; you're just making sure that your intuition and personal perceptions aren't being pushed aside by excessive reasoning and overthinking.* Thinking simply opens the way for us to regain the strength and clarity that are lost through making life more complicated than it needs to be.

Now before you dismiss that last statement—and maybe the rest of the book—let me be clear: Life is hard, and challenges *are* complex. Your plate may be so full right now that there's no room for a fork. Maybe you're dealing with a rebellious teen, a parent's terminal illness, the foreclosure of your home, or even all three.

> **The man who has understanding has everything.**
>
> JEWISH PROVERB

Under no circumstances are we minimizing or dismissing the difficulties you face on a daily basis. My point isn't that life is easy but rather that when you analyze and re-analyze your problems in an attempt to solve them, you actually lose clarity instead of gain it and are unable to appropriate the resources you need in order to deal with life as you know it.

So if too much thinking gets in the way of finding solutions, where do we find the clarity we need? When Josh Waitzkin was stuck in a chess game, he found the solution when he imagined the chessboard cleared of its pieces. In the same way, a clear head makes it easier to see wisely.

THE POWER OF A CLEAR HEAD

On a summer Saturday afternoon, Gary Klein, a cognitive psychologist, sat in a fire station in Cleveland, Ohio, waiting for the alarm to sound. Klein explores how people think, and he believes that people dismiss too readily the power of gut instinct. Here's how one writer described a scenario from Klein's research:

Klein and his research team are attempting to crack a mystery that has intrigued psychologists for decades: How do people who work in unpredictable situations make life-and-death decisions? And how do they do it so well? According to decision-making models, they should fail more often than they succeed. There is too much uncertainty and too little time for them to make good choices. Yet again and again, they do the right thing. Klein wants to know why.

At 3:21 PM, the alarm goes off. Klein, an assistant, and an emergency-rescue crew scramble aboard an EMS truck. Three minutes later, they pull up to a house in a suburban neighborhood. A man is lying facedown on the front lawn. Blood is pooling all around him. He slipped on a ladder and pushed his arm through a plate-glass window, slicing an artery. The head of the rescue team—Klein calls him "Lieutenant M"—quickly estimates that the man has already lost two units of blood. If he loses two more, he'll die.

Even as he leaps from the truck, the lieutenant knows by judging the amount of blood on the ground that the man has ripped an artery. In an instant, he applies pressure to the man's arm. Emergency-medical procedure dictates that the victim should be checked for other injuries before he is moved. But there isn't time. The lieutenant orders his crew members to get the man into the truck. As the vehicle races to the hospital, a crew member puts inflatable pants on the victim to stabilize his blood pressure. This marks another real-time judgment call: Had they put the pants on the victim before moving him, the crew would have lost precious seconds.

The ambulance pulls up to the hospital's ER. Klein looks at his watch: It's 3:31 PM. In a matter of minutes, the lieutenant made several critical decisions that ultimately saved the man's life. But he ignored the conventional rules of decision making. He didn't ponder the best course of action or weigh his options. He didn't rely on deductive thinking or on an analysis of probabilities. How did he know what to do? When Klein asked him, the lieutenant shrugged and said that he simply drew on his experience.[7]

After more than two decades of studying cases like this, Klein had concluded that the lieutenant harnessed his inherent intuition. His instinctual perceptions allowed him to cut through the complexities of time pressure, high stakes, personal responsibilities, and shifting conditions. He wasn't thinking through procedures, and he certainly wasn't swayed by emotions; he was working with a clear head and going with his gut. In Klein's words, the lieutenant's intuition infused his work with power.[8]

DO YOU HAVE THE SACRED GIFT?

Intuition—that effortless, immediate, unreasoned sense of truth—has a strange reputation. Skilled decision makers know that they can depend on their intuition, but at the same time they may feel uncomfortable trusting a source of power that seems so unintended or maybe even ethereal.

When Klein asked the fire-fighting lieutenant how he knew just what to do when he saw the man with a torn artery lying in his front yard, he shrugged and said he didn't know. Intuition is like that. It's often inexplicable. In fact, experts say that intuition is recognizing things without knowing how we do the recognizing.

For curious reasons, we are drawn to certain cues and not others within our awareness. Although they seem to emerge from an obscure inner force, they actually begin with a perception of something outside—a facial expression, a tone of voice, a visual inconsistency so fleeting that we're not even aware we noticed.[9] But as a result, we somehow know what goals to pursue, what to expect, and how to respond.

> God, grant me the serenity to accept the things I cannot change, the courage to change the things I can, and the wisdom to know the difference.
>
> REINHOLD NIEBUHR

Consider a Formula 1 driver who braked sharply when nearing a hairpin turn without knowing why—and as a result avoided hitting a pileup of cars on the track ahead, undoubtedly saving his life.

"The driver couldn't explain why he felt he should stop, but the urge was much stronger than his desire to win the race," explains Professor G. P. Hodgkinson of Leeds University. "The driver underwent forensic analysis by psychologists afterwards, where he was shown a video to mentally relive the event. In hindsight he realized that the crowd, which would have normally been cheering him on, wasn't looking at him coming up to the bend but was looking the other way in a static, frozen way. That was the cue. He didn't consciously process this, but he knew something was wrong and stopped in time."[10]

According to Hodgkinson, intuition is the result of the way our brains store, process, and retrieve information on a subconscious level. In other words, our intuition taps into information that is underneath our conscious awareness. When we overthink, we prevent our intuitive minds from doing their work.

By the way, you don't have to drive race cars to experience this phenomenon. Try asking a gourmet cook how she knows to do things that aren't in the recipe or how she can cook a fantastic dish without a recipe at all. She can't explain it. Try asking people who have an intuition about knowing they've met the person they are going to marry when it's been only a few days. They will tell you they "just know" and nothing more. It's what led philosopher Blaise Pascal to say, "The heart has reasons which reason does not know."

Some people think of intuition as an inborn trait that some people get and others don't. But scientists disagree. They don't see just some people as being blessed with intuition. They say all of us hold an intuitive capacity. They say intuition grows within *all* of us. And all of us can access this part of ourselves if we learn to clear our minds.

Those who say they lack intuition are essentially paralyzed, because they are relying exclusively on their rational minds. Psychologist Antoine Bechara, at the University of Southern California, studied brain-damaged patients who could not form emotional intuitions when making a decision. They were left to decide through purely deliberate reasoning. "They ended up doing such a complicated analysis, factoring everything in, that it could take them hours to decide between two kinds of cereal," Bechara says.[11]

Let's face it: We need to access our intuitive minds if we are to move forward in our lives. This "sacred gift," as Albert Einstein called it, is a major source of strength. So how do we access that gift?

> It is in lonely solitude that God delivers his best thoughts, and the mind needs to be still and quiet to receive them.
>
> CHARLES R. SWINDOLL

LISTENING TO THAT STILL, SMALL VOICE

When Albert Einstein labeled the intuitive mind a sacred gift, he was commenting on its spiritual implications. To ignore the spiritual profundity of the insightful whispers we hear in our intuitive minds is to miss out on their potential power.

But is Einstein right? Could it be that divine guidance actually comes to us through our intuitive minds? Could those unreasoned moments really be heavenly whispers?

Here's what science tells us: If God is on our minds, if we think about relating to God over time, our brains make some surprising changes. Literally. Neural functioning actually begins to alter. It turns out that being "transformed by the renewing of your mind" is more than metaphorical.[12] Neurological renewal occurs when we focus on God: "Different circuits become activated, while others become deactivated. New dendrites are formed, new synaptic connections are made, and the brain becomes more sensitive to subtle realms of experience."[13] That's right. The more we relate to God, the more our brains become attuned to hearing that "still, small voice."

> One of the highest and noblest functions of man's mind is to listen to God, and so to read his mind, and think his thoughts after him.
>
> JOHN R. W. STOTT

But here's the hitch: You have to have a clear head if you want to hear clearly from God's Spirit. That is, you have to relax the tension around your overthinking in order to make room for your intuition. The word *intuition* comes from the Latin word *intueri*, which is roughly translated as "to contemplate." So your intuition stems from what you are considering, what you are attuned to. If you want to hear from God, you've got to be attuned to his Spirit. When you are, you can become sensitive to the sacred gift of God's whispers.

If you're not attuned to God, you miss out on the sacred gift. John, the author of several biblical writings, puts it bluntly: "He who belongs to God hears what God says. The reason you do not hear is that you do not belong to God."[14] It's echoed many times throughout the pages of the Bible: "The person who is joined to the Lord is one spirit with him."[15]

The bottom line is this: You can derive amazing power and strength in your life when God speaks to you through your intuitive mind. But the complexities of your rational mind—with all its worries, obsessions, and fears—often keep your intuitive mind shut down. God wants to speak to you through your mind, but you've got to clear your head to hear his sacred whispers.

IF THE DEVIL IS IN THE DETAILS, GOD IS IN THE BIG PICTURE

When Gary Klein was conducting his research at the Cleveland fire station, he noticed that when the most experienced commanders confronted a fire, the biggest question they had to deal with wasn't, What do I do? but, What's going on? In other words, they looked at the big picture. That's what their experience buys them. They aren't hurriedly wondering what procedure to follow or what technique to use; they have their wits about them as they survey the scene. They are contemplating, within an instant, what is happening so that their actions come from understanding. In a word, they are approaching the scene with wisdom.

It's the same for those of us who seek God. We don't have to scuttle through life wondering what to do next. We are aware of God's ways, and our attunement, our focus on God, guides our actions. We ask ourselves, *What's going on with God here?*

Too often, in an attempt to follow God, we get hung up on *doing* godly things: attending church, reading the Bible, giving money, volunteering our time, and all the rest. But we don't hear God's Spirit speaking into our minds because our minds are too cluttered. We're so busy *doing* that we don't take time to *be*. And then, when we are finally still long enough to contemplate God, we wonder why we're not more clearly aware of God's speaking.[16]

But if we're honest, we *do* know why. A recent survey of more than twenty thousand Christians between the ages of fifteen and eighty-eight found that busyness is the greatest challenge we face in attuning to God. Sixty percent say that it's "often" or "always" true that "the busyness of life gets in the way of developing my relationship with God." And when pastors respond to that question, the result bumps up to 65 percent.[17]

So what can we do? How can we calm the chaos and complexity in our hurried heads? The answer is actually quite simple. It's found in this short sentence: "Be still, and know that I am God!"[18]

I can almost hear you asking, "How in the world can I be still when life is so fast?" That's a fair question. God does not expect us to be contemplative monks in order to hear his inner voice. He merely asks that we be attuned to his presence—even in the calamity and chaos of our lives. Being still does not necessarily mean retreating to a quiet place. It means quieting our minds, even in the midst of chaos, by not trying to figure everything out. It means not striving so hard. It means putting our minds at ease and letting God be God. It means seeing the big picture.

KNOWING WHEN TO TAKE OFF YOUR SHOES

"We may ignore, but we can nowhere evade, the presence of God. The world is crowded with Him. He walks everywhere incognito," wrote C. S. Lewis in *Letters to Malcolm*. Lewis, of course, did not mean that it's a game of trying to figure out where God is. Quite the contrary. God is everywhere, even in the most common of places, when we quiet our minds enough to notice. You see, the complexity of our rational minds—so often troubled with deadlines, worries, tasks, and drives—keeps us looking down. It forces us to focus, almost exclusively, on our own stories. It prevents us from looking up to see the bigger story. And the bigger story, the story of all stories, is that God is God.

For some reason, we have a tough time remembering that. Whenever we overthink our own stories, we narrow our personal perspectives. Our vision shrinks. We focus on questions such as, What's happening to me? instead of asking, What's God doing here? Our narrow outlook limits what *could* be, and instead, we complicate the situation and busy ourselves with what *should* be. In short, we forget to be still and know that God is God.

"Earth's crammed with heaven, and every common bush afire with God," said Elizabeth Barrett Browning. "But only he who sees takes off his shoes; the rest sit round and pick blackberries." Isn't it true? Don't you feel that you're sometimes missing out on God's dramatic movement because you aren't sensitive to the holy ground you're walking on? Oblivious to what God could be doing, we miss the spectacular signs of his activity because we're overly focused on the details and complications of our own lives.

Of course, it's not always easy to see and hear God in the common places. Our myopic vision sees to that. And relaxing our minds enough to let God be God is unquestionably challenging. That's why even as a sincere God-follower you unknowingly end up walking over holy ground on your way to pick blackberries, never realizing what could have happened if you had taken off your proverbial shoes.

> **The difference between worldliness and godliness is a renewed mind.**
>
> ERWIN W. LUTZER

The only thing that makes these efforts easier is wisdom.[19] Of course, that's a tall order. Thomas Carlyle said wisdom is the highest achievement of humankind. So don't expect it to come overnight. But you *can* expect it. Wisdom is the by-product of routinely, over time, clearing your head. And the holy moments you experience with God are moments of wisdom. The more you experience, the more wisdom you acquire. Soon you'll have a history of sacred moments with God, and you'll be proficient at hearing his whispers.

Try this: When your mind is filled with the clutter of

overthinking—ask God for wisdom. It sounds too simple, I know. But I urge you to ask. In fact, ask boldly, without a second thought. And make it a habit. The invitation is as clear as day: "If any of you lacks wisdom, he should ask God, who gives generously."[20]

I can easily fall into the routine of coming home from lecturing at the university at the end of the day and unknowingly walk over "holy ground" in the playroom of our home where my two little boys are huddled around a project of building with their blocks. Why? Because I'm on my way to check my e-mail, never realizing what might have happened if I'd taken off my proverbial—or maybe literal—shoes and knelt down on the floor to connect with my kids. But if, before walking into our home's front door, I whisper a clarifying prayer, asking God for wisdom, I can tell you that my head is almost sure to clear and I'm not about to miss out on the sacred moment on the floor with my two little boys.

When you clear your head—when you still your rational mind enough to make room for your intuitive mind—you're creating space for God to give you wisdom. And as you acquire wisdom, you begin to integrate knowledge, experience, and deep understanding. You learn to tolerate the uncertainties of life as well as its ups and downs. You have an awareness of how things play out over time and of how God can help you make sense of them. Wise people generally share an optimism that keeps them moving forward, and they experience a certain amount of calm when facing difficult decisions. In other words, they see the big picture.

Consider Tami. She's suffered more hardship than anyone should ever have to endure. Her father died when she was in her teens. Her mother suffered from debilitating depression. Tami's marriage to a verbally abusive man ended after six years because he had an affair with another woman. Yet in spite of these jolts, Tami made choices to keep moving forward with her life by learning from her experiences. In fact, as a single mom, she learned to

YOU'RE STRONGER THAN YOU THINK

leverage her past to help others and managed to earn a degree in counseling. Today, she's a wise and trusted counselor in Seattle, with a waiting list of clients who want to see her. Why? Because Tami, more than most, embodies a quiet confidence and can see the big picture.

The English word *wisdom* is derived from an old Anglo-Saxon word meaning "to see." And in Greek, the word for wisdom means "clear." Wisdom is what enables us to see the big picture. Wisdom is what enables us to "see" God.

So, wisdom is the bridge between your cluttered, harried mind and the deeper yearnings of your God-given spirit. Take off your shoes as you cross over that bridge, for you will be on holy ground.

GIVE PEACE A CHANCE

You may have heard of the political doctrine of achieving "peace through strength." But for God-followers, it's the other way around: Strength comes through peace. God promises that when you are feeling your weakest, when you are broken and frail, he will keep you in "perfect peace" when your mind is focused on him. Why? Because, as the prophet Isaiah said, "The Lord God is the eternal Rock."[21] God is your strength. As I close this chapter on thinking simply, I leave you with a simple story about a king and a painting contest.

> You will keep in perfect peace all who trust in you, all whose thoughts are fixed on you! Trust in the Lnqc always, for the Lnqc Gnc is the eternal Rock.
>
> ISAIAH 26:3-4

The king was building a new palace, and he wanted the main entrance hall to be decorated with a large work of art. The king envisioned his kingdom as a peaceful land, so whoever's painting best symbolized peace would win a large cash prize.

Over the next few months, hundreds of paintings arrived at

the palace. The king decided on the top two. Before announcing a winner, he hung both paintings in the palace for public viewing.

The first painting was of a majestic lake, so tranquil and still that the lush hills behind it were perfectly mirrored in its reflection. The sky was a brilliant blue with soft, puffy clouds floating above. Wildflowers bursting with color outlined the lake, and a family of deer calmly grazed in a far meadow. All who saw it felt peace and happiness.

The second painting portrayed a tall mountain cliff, rugged and strong. A few small trees grew out of the cracks of the face of the cliff, with gnarled roots clinging for life. A foamy waterfall angrily crashed down the cliff and into the misty abyss. Above, ominous clouds loomed, and in the distance, lightning flashed. Halfway up the cliff grew a small bush. In its branches, a bird sat in a nest, apparently warming her eggs.

After several weeks, the king declared the second painting the winner. Confused, the people asked the king to explain his decision. He explained that peace is not the absence of conflict but rather a state of mind, and that those who experience peace have clarity and calm even when turmoil surrounds them.

That's the point. You're stronger than you know because you can have peace of mind. That peace doesn't depend on the weather. It doesn't depend on anyone else. It doesn't depend on your income, your job, or the economy. It doesn't depend on everything going your way. It doesn't even depend on your health. Whatever your circumstances, you can make the way for a peace that transcends understanding—even in the midst of confusion and complexity—by clearing the proverbial chessboard of your mind to see how God wants to move in the big picture of your life.

FOR REFLECTION

1. Do you identify with the idea of sometimes overthinking your situation? When are you most prone to do that, and why?

2. Can you recall a time when you heard the still, small voice of God in the midst of your hurried life? If so, what were you doing, and what enabled you to hear it?

3. How do you feel about asking God for wisdom? Consider a specific time and place when you think you could do this. How might it help you clear your head?

4. What difference would it make in your life if you could experience deep peace in the midst of confusion and complication? In what area of your life would you like to experience that peace right now?

WORKBOOK EXERCISE 1

A Brief Note on the Workbook: If you are looking for a tool to help you personally apply what you are learning, the You're Stronger Than You Think Workbook *contains a variety of exercises and self-tests for each chapter in this book. Having the workbook is not required. It is merely an option if you'd like to use it. The workbook is available separately at bookstores and online at www.LesandLeslie.com.*

If you are using the workbook in conjunction with your reading, the first exercise will reveal what, in specific terms, tends to cloud your mind. It will help you pinpoint those situations in which you are most likely to overthink, and it will reveal what you can do, in personal terms, to curb this tendency. It will also help you locate the areas in your life where you will find the deepest benefits of tapping into your intuitive mind so that you can more clearly hear the sacred gift of God's whispers in your life.

2
THINK EXPECTANTLY
THERE'S STRENGTH
IN ANTICIPATION

What oxygen is to the lungs,
such is hope to the meaning of life.
—Emil Brunner

I would never in my wildest imagination have expected to hear that Bill Dallas, my friend of ten years, had been a prisoner in San Quentin.

We were both speaking at a leadership conference in Orange County, California. I had just come off the stage after giving my remarks. Lou Holtz, the famed football coach, was speaking next. Then Bill took the stage and had the house deathly still as he told his dramatic story.

It started in the late 1980s with some shady financial decisions Bill made as a high-flying real-estate entrepreneur. Those decisions took him from the very top of life to the absolute bottom. He lost the trust of everyone. He lost his friends. He lost his family. He nearly lost himself. It's no exaggeration to say that Bill's life literally fell apart.

Bill was convicted of grand theft embezzlement and found

himself living with "the worst of the worst" in prison—and contemplating suicide. Bill talked about how he was literally curled up in the fetal position on the filth of the walled-in prison yard when he realized just how low he had fallen—from a powerful role as CEO in San Francisco to a convicted felon in San Quentin.

When he first got to prison, Bill could only see the walls— thick, unassailable walls. Everywhere he turned were barricades, fences, and obstructions. But the biggest barriers Bill faced were not visible to anyone else. They were in his head. And those walls were starting to close in around him.

> **Hope is the word which God has written on the brow of every man.**
>
> VICTOR HUGO

Bill described the stuffy prison bus as it rolled through the exterior gate and then moved inside the walls of San Quentin. He found he couldn't take his eyes off the windowless, seventy-foot-high, yard-thick, steel and concrete walls. They seemed to have been built to convey a single message to prisoners: *You are not getting out of here.*

Once off the bus, in shackles, Bill shuffled to the "reception" block of the least desirable of all state prisons, and a hard-nosed corrections officer (known to prisoners as a CO) barked orders and issued him an orange jumpsuit, the attire of a newbie before getting the denim blue uniform. Just days earlier he had been wearing a crisp shirt and a tailored suit. Bill said losing his wardrobe was nothing compared to losing his identity as a person. To the California Department of Corrections, Bill was now H64741. For all intents and purposes, Bill Dallas no longer existed. He was now a number, living for the next three years in a dingy, dimly lit cell with concrete walls so close together that it felt like a coffin.

That day, February 1, 1993, Bill became a true prisoner— both physically and, even worse, mentally. All hope was gone, or so he thought.

Two years into his prison sentence, something almost inexplicable happened. For reasons you're about to discover in this chapter, Bill stopped seeing the walls. It was a breakthrough. He had a new perspective. It had nothing to do with knowing his parole was closer. It wasn't about Bill's eventual freedom outside the walls of San Quentin. It was about the freedom outside the walls within his own head—even though the physical walls remained.

"I STOPPED SEEING THE WALLS"

When Bill used that sentence in his talk, I felt as if his words were in italics. I knew exactly what he meant. I've seen it numerous times in my counseling office. When people are hemmed in by the walls of their past, the walls of their fears, the walls of their insecurities, the walls of disappointments, the walls of whatever— they can't see beyond their current predicaments. And as a result they lose all perspective. All they see are hurdles and obstacles to living the lives they had imagined.

> Hope is the feeling that the feeling you have isn't permanent.
>
> JEAN KERR

But once their mental walls come down, whether gradually or in a sudden tumble, they see options that had previously eluded them. They see opportunities they had been missing. They see hope where they didn't think it existed.

Lewis Smedes was among my favorite professors when I was in graduate school. And Lew loved hope. He'd often say it was bred in the bone. We can't live without hope. When we keep hoping, we keep living. When we stop hoping, we die. Inside.

We all need hope because we all feel anxious at times. We all struggle and suffer on occasion. We all long for something better. We all have unfulfilled dreams. And we are all headed into a future over which we have no control. Life is uncertain for everyone. One way or another, all of us hunger for hope. And that's precisely why we can all find power in "not seeing the walls." We don't have to be prison inmates to understand that. Each of us builds mental walls that make us weaker.

Some of us conjure up unrealistic fears about failing at work and suffer paralyzing anxiety as a result. The woman who sabotages her relationships because she was burned early on by a boyfriend is another example. She puts up emotional walls that keep anyone from getting close. Others are convinced they can never pursue advanced education because no one in their families has ever attended college. The number of walls people build are as numerous as people on the planet.

And that's why I dedicate this chapter to helping you, whatever your "walls" might be, find the strength that comes from anticipation. In the previous chapter we talked about thinking simply. In this chapter we talk about thinking expectantly.

THE POWER OF POSITIVE EXPECTATIONS

One of the classic early studies of expectancy was conducted by Robert Rosenthal, professor emeritus at Harvard.[1] He told elementary school teachers that a test had identified some of their students as "intellectual bloomers." The teachers were told the names of those students and were led to expect that those students would do particularly well in the coming academic year.

In fact, the information the teachers received was bogus. The students identified as bloomers were no different academically from the other students. Their names were selected at random. Only their teachers' expectations for them differed. Yet, sure enough, by the end of the school year, the students who were expected to bloom really had performed better, significantly better, than the other students.[2]

Some years later, another research team performed a similar

experiment, but this time they focused on the students' expectations of their teachers. One group of students was told their teacher was "quite effective," and another group was told their teacher was "incompetent." This time the teachers knew nothing about the study. The results showed that students with negative expectations rated the lessons "more difficult, less interesting, and less effective." They also scored lower on their exams than the other group. Students with positive expectations leaned forward more in their chairs and had better eye contact with the teacher, in addition to having higher test scores.[3]

It's difficult to dispute: Expectations have a powerful influence on learning outcomes. But the research on expectations goes far beyond education. These studies were conducted decades ago. By now, the power of expectations has been clearly demonstrated not just in classrooms but also in workplaces, courtrooms, the military, doctors' offices, parent-child interactions, counseling, consumer transactions, and more. The bottom line is that our expectations have an impact on our reality and create self-fulfilling prophecies as a result.[4]

> How we believe the world is and what we honestly think it can become have powerful effects on how things turn out.
>
> JAMES RHEM

Rosenthal's research and the numerous studies that followed underscore the power of expectations—especially when the expectations are focused on people around us. But what about the expectations we place on ourselves? Do they also hold the power to alter our lives?

THE GREAT DISCOVERY

A man was traveling across the country by sneaking rides on freight trains. One particular night he climbed into what looked like a boxcar and closed the door. With the jolt of the train, the door locked shut, and he was trapped inside. As his eyes adjusted to the darkness, he must have noticed how chilly it was and then discovered he was inside a refrigerated boxcar. He probably hollered for help and pounded the walls, but his noise failed to attract anyone's attention. The man eventually gave up and lay down on the floor of the railroad car, shivering.

Evidently believing he would soon freeze to death, he scratched part of a message on the floor of the car. He never finished. Sometime late the next day, a repairman from the railroad opened the door of the boxcar and found the man dead. He appeared to have frozen to death. But the reason for the repairman's arrival was that the refrigeration units on the car were not working. The temperature inside the car never went below fifty degrees during the night—not nearly cold enough to kill a man. So why did the man die? Because he *expected* to freeze to death.[5]

Okay, you think, *but this is just one dramatic anecdote communicators use to illustrate a point.* That may be so. But consider another example that is well documented in the research literature, one that has been replicated in different forms tens of thousands of times.

Nearly fifty years ago, a team of doctors reported a single incident that stunned medical researchers. It had to do with a Mr. Wright, who was suffering from cancer of the lymph system and had developed large tumors throughout his body. At the time, a group of physicians were studying a new chemical formula called Krebiozen, which was being widely touted by the media as a miracle cure for cancer, although the medical establishment was less convinced. Wright's cancer was so far advanced that the physicians gave him the drug only as a compassionate exception—not because they expected any response. However, what happened next seemed nearly miraculous. Wright gained weight and looked and felt better, and his tumors shrank so drastically that they could hardly be detected.

Wright's improvement continued until the newspapers began reporting that Krebiozen was not the great advance they had first thought. After reading the negative coverage, Wright became discouraged and immediately began to lose weight, and his tumors grew once more.

But the story doesn't end there. Mr. Wright's physicians quickly recognized the power of his expectations and decided to influence them. They told him that the first batches of Krebiozen had not been at full potency. The lab had corrected the problem, they assured him, and the new, stronger batch of the drug would soon be on its way. They continued to encourage Wright's hopes and finally announced that the big day was here—the new batch of the drug had arrived. They then proceeded to give Wright injections just as before, but they actually injected only sterile water.

Wright showed the same dramatic improvements that had occurred with the Krebiozen. His remission lasted until, for a second time, the newspapers undermined the physicians—stating unequivocally, "AMA reports that Krebiozen is worthless against cancer." Mr. Wright once again began to sink, his tumors grew massive, and shortly thereafter, he died.[6]

If you want proof that your personal expectations matter, you need look no further than what we now call the placebo effect. It definitively shows that what we expect of ourselves holds unbridled power. Abundant medical research has proven that what we think commands the brain to produce unassailable changes in the body's chemistry, either setting the stage for intensified illness or quicker recovery.[7] So it stands to reason that if what we say in our brains can influence our bodies, then what we say in our brains can have an impact on other areas of our lives as well. If our expectations influence our physical well-being, in other words, imagine the impact they have on our emotional health.

Actually, you need not imagine it at all. For decades, the

impact of anticipatory thinking on our emotions has been studied from every angle, researched across cultures, and documented in countless scholarly journals and numerous professional presentations.[8] A mountain of research has shown us that what you expect, what you anticipate, powerfully affects not only what you feel but whether you succeed in meeting your goals. One of America's pioneering psychologists, William James, said that our capacity to alter our lives simply by altering the expectations of our minds is "the great discovery."[9]

WHAT DO YOU EXPECT?

Now, before you start ratcheting up your personal expectations, let's consider the implications. Some have taken this notion of finding strength through positive anticipation as an amazing "secret" of the cosmos.[10] *If I just change my thoughts*, they think, *I can have it all.* They claim that focused positive thinking can result in increased wealth, health, happiness, and more. Sounds pretty good, right? All you have to do is believe firmly enough in the inevitability of your success, and you will have it. But could raising our expectations of life and ourselves—expecting to attract whatever we want to us—be setting us up with false hope?

> Success is not final, failure is not fatal: it is the courage to continue that counts.
>
> WINSTON CHURCHILL

You probably know someone who had positive expectations for losing weight, for example, but didn't meet with success. You might know someone who had positive expectations about a financial plan that didn't turn out well. You probably know someone who has been expecting to find "Mr./Ms. Right" for years . . . and is still waiting. You get the idea. Positive expectations, while undeniably powerful, aren't as straightforward as we might be tempted to believe. After all, isn't the trite phrase "Expect the unexpected" true? Aren't we bound to have times when we are caught off guard? Of course. Even the most fervent believers in "the secret" wouldn't argue that.

So, could it be that hope and positive expectations aren't all we want them to be?

THE TRUTH BEHIND FALSE HOPE

False hope is the ultimate tool of deception. New Year's resolutions are an obvious example. We resolve to keep our cool, start a business, save our money, write a book, lose weight, overcome an addiction, or learn a healthier behavior. About 45 percent of us make resolutions—often the same ones year after year. Why do we so often fail to keep them? Experts point to unrealistic expectations that produce false hope. We falsely fantasize that things will change, even though our histories show repeated failure. Our failure begins with exaggerated feelings of control and overconfidence about our ability to change our behaviors successfully. We often start out with an idealistic goal (e.g., "I will exercise for at least one hour every day!"), and we expect dramatic, rapid results (e.g., "I'll lose about five pounds a week"). When the new behavior proves to be more difficult than we anticipated, and when results come more slowly than we expected, we often abandon our attempts to change.

> Those who trust in the LNQC will find new strength. They will soar high on wings like eagles. They will run and not grow weary. They will walk and not faint.
>
> ISAIAH 40:31

But why do we keep trying again and again to achieve the same goals? Because we explain our failures in ways that maintain that false hope for the future. For instance, we blame ourselves for not trying hard enough (e.g., "If only I try a bit harder next time, I'm sure I'll succeed"). We may also blame external circumstances for our failures and decide that these circumstances are unlikely to occur again (e.g., "I won't be as busy next year as I have been this year, so I'll have more time to exercise"). So we remain hopeful that we'll succeed on our next attempt. We convince ourselves that this diet will be easier than the one we tried last year, or this kind of exercise will be less boring than using a stationary bicycle. Unfortunately, the new strategy is often no easier, no more effective, or no less boring than the last one, and we fail again.

Of course, it's not just New Year's resolutions that can engender false hope. We can become deluded by false hope when faced with a troubling diagnosis, a dead-end relationship, a history of abuse with a spouse, or a dream that requires competencies we lack.

Our personal hopes and expectations can disappoint us. They can lead us on. They can tease us with desires that are seemingly and perpetually beyond our reach. So should we lower our expectations? Is that the remedy for eliminating the pain and frustration? Should we stifle our wishes, quiet our dreams, and hinder our hopes? Hardly. "To hope is to risk frustration," said Thomas Merton. "Therefore, make up your mind to risk frustration." In other words, we need to go into hope wide-eyed. We need to know that our hopes can hurt. False hope brings pain. There's no way around it.

But sometimes a hope fulfilled is just as dangerous.

WHEN YOUR DREAMS COME TRUE

"Be careful what you wish for," your mother may have said. "Question your desires," warned Theseus in Shakespeare's *A Midsummer Night's Dream*. "You must not covet," commands the Torah.[11] Why all these warnings? Is the fulfillment of our hopes a recipe for disappointment? It is for some.

Ask lottery winners, for example. After expecting money to make them happy, about 70 percent of them would gladly give it all back if they could undo the havoc it wreaked on their lives. Sadly, this 70 percent end up getting divorced and have serious family feuds within a few years of winning their financial windfall.[12]

Ask a third of all people who successfully climb the corporate ladder. "You think when a person goes up the ladder, they somehow become more self-assured. But it's precisely the opposite," says John Kolligian, a university psychologist who has studied self-doubt following success.[13] These high achievers are unable to overcome intense self-criticism, and they feel like imposters. As a result they suffer from anxiety, insecurity, and depression.

Irish author Oscar Wilde once wrote, "In this world there are only two tragedies. One is not getting what one wants, and the other is getting it." Deep down, our greatest hope is not for fame, comfort, wealth, or power. Those rewards create almost as many problems as they solve. If we reach our goals, if our dreams come true, we're bound to wake up someday and ask, "Is this it?"

> **Where there is no vision, there is no hope.**
>
> GEORGE WASHINGTON CARVER

We will never be happy or fulfilled until we stop measuring our real-life achievements against the dream of whatever we imagined would make us happy. Daniel Levinson calls that the "tyranny of the Dream."[14] Each of us developed this dream when we were young. Maybe it was planted by parents or teachers, or maybe it came from our own imaginings. The Dream was to someday be truly special. We dreamed that our work would be recognized, that our marriages would be perfect and our children exemplary. We may have dared to dream we'd be famous or affluent. And if we've been hit by a major jolt—diagnosed with cancer, for example—our Dream has been deferred while we hope for a cure. But whatever we are dreaming of, we keep holding out hope that one day it will be realized and the fairy tale will be complete. But, as Anaïs Nin reminds us, "We've been poisoned by fairytales." They don't come true. The Dream can never make us happy. Even if we reach our goals to become the success we imagined, we're likely to feel empty. Why emptiness? Because our greatest hope is not for fame, comfort, wealth, or power. These are shallow hopes. Our greatest hope is far deeper. Whether we know it or not, our greatest hope is for meaning.

GREAT EXPECTATIONS

"Hope is not the conviction that something will turn out well," said the late Czech writer and statesman Václav Havel, "but the certainty that something makes sense, regardless of how it turns out." He was talking about meaning. He was talking about a life that matters even when that life doesn't measure up to the Dream— and even when that dream becomes our worst nightmare.

Before we unpack this idea, I want to be clear about one thing: A disposition of positive expectation is a valuable asset. Creating goals and anticipating desirable outcomes are essential to moving forward and making a contribution in this life. Optimistic people who hold on to hope achieve more, help more, and enjoy more than those who don't. "There is no medicine like hope," said writer and publisher Orison Marden, "no incentive so great, and no tonic so powerful as expectation of something better tomorrow." I couldn't agree more.

But the deeper our hopes, the more satisfying and meaningful are our lives. The realization of a shallow hope simply reveals how vapid the hope was to begin with. It's short-lived and thin as vapor, as King Solomon would have said. And if we hold out false hope that it is going to truly fulfill us, only to encounter continual disappointment, we will eventually shake our fists to the heavens and say, like the writer of Ecclesiastes, "Everything is meaningless!"[15]

Hope, according to Lewis Smedes, is made up of three ingredients: First, there's a *desire* for something to be different. Second is the *belief* that it can happen. And third is the *worry* that it won't. That's the rub. Our beliefs need convincing. We fear the possibility that what we hope for may not happen, and the greater our fears, the less hope we have. That's why human hope is always risky—or is it?

There is one hope—one great expectation—that trumps all others. It is a hope that does not disappoint. It infuses our dreams with purpose and significance. And it's the source of the true strength of anticipation.

A HOPE THAT DOES NOT DISAPPOINT

The word *disappoint* comes from French and originally meant "to remove from office." It goes back to the days when a monarch would appoint or disappoint an officer. To be "disappointed" was to lose one's post. These days, it means to lose one's hope. Disappointments can result from big setbacks, like getting a dire diagnosis, or from small mishaps, like not getting an upgrade on a long flight. They are a part of life. We can learn to manage our disappointments, but as long as hope is alive, we cannot eliminate them.

So how could there be a hope that does *not* disappoint? It is a hope that has its basis in faith.[16] And faith changes everything. "Faith is the confidence that what we hope for will actually happen," said one biblical writer.[17] It moves worry to the backstage of hope. Faith emboldens our beliefs and expectations with confidence. Faith can make us fearless. "Hope is hearing the melody of the future," said Rubem Alves. "Faith is to dance to it."

> When you say a situation or a person is hopeless, you are slamming the door in the face of God.
>
> CHARLES L. ALLEN

How does faith do this mystical work? By giving us an eternal perspective. People of faith look at life differently. Hope-filled optimism about our future, when bolstered by faith, moderates our anxiety about the present. We look at life through a bigger lens. Viewing life's problems through the big lens of the future helps put in perspective today's aggravations—car troubles, family quarrels, delayed flights. So many of the things that once riled us can now be seen as what they are: trivial, temporary irritants.

But faith goes deeper than helping us cope with mere aggravations. The true power of faith is seen most clearly in times of pain. Faith turns hope into a certainty that suffering will make sense even when our earthly perspective can see it only as senseless. In other words, when pain cuts us to the core and hardships punch us in the solar plexus, faith is responsible for keeping our hope alive.

WHEN HOPE TAKES HER LAST BREATH

I have to admit that I sometimes have to hold on to faith by my fingernails. My faith doesn't seem to put all my doubts to bed. In fact, in my experience, doubt is a close companion of faith. French theologian Jacques Ellul had it right: "The person who is plunged into doubt is not the unbeliever but the person who has no other hope but hope." Unbelievers do not have to doubt. Believers doubt precisely because they live by faith and not by sight. I mention my struggle only to reassure other strugglers that they have company—and to tell you that I find strength in expectancy when I hear stories of other people's faith. People like Nancy Guthrie. Maybe you will too.

Nancy knew her baby had problems almost immediately, but she and her husband named the baby girl Hope. Born with clubfeet and extreme lethargy, among other problems, Hope was officially diagnosed with Zellweger Syndrome. There is no treatment or cure for this rare metabolic disorder. Most babies with the disease live fewer than six months.

As Nancy looked at Hope, she thought, *Here's my chance to*

respond to the worst thing I can imagine in a way that is pleasing to God. It wasn't easy. Nancy had to make that decision over and over again during the next few months. Her grieving didn't get easier. Hope wasn't healed. The pain didn't lessen. But each day, Nancy trusted God to do something meaningful despite her loneliness and grief.

On Hope's 199th day, she took her last breath. But that was not the end of Nancy's hope.

Both parents must be carriers of a particular recessive gene for Zellweger Syndrome to occur. The Guthries decided David would have a vasectomy to prevent another pregnancy. Only one in two thousand vasectomies fails, so the couple felt secure. But one year after Hope died, Nancy was pregnant again. Prenatal testing revealed this child would also have Zellweger Syndrome.

Time magazine interviewed Nancy and David for an article in which the writer compared their plight to that of Job's in the Old Testament. The article quotes an entry from Nancy's journal: "[Like Job], we often cannot see the hidden purposes of God, but we can determine to be faithful and keep walking toward Him in the darkness."[18]

Gabriel, named after the angel, was born on July 16, 2001. The Guthries knew what to expect. Their son's first day would be his best. Gabriel died 183 days later. Nancy says that answering how or why begins with another question: What? What do I believe about God? "Do I trust God enough to believe he's in control and whatever he allows in my life will be for my ultimate good—not that whatever he allows in my life is good?" Nancy has commented.[19]

> **Hope is passion for what is possible.**
> SØREN KIERKEGAARD

It has been said that faith isn't faith until it's all you're holding on to. Nancy's hope had left her clinging to nothing more than a conviction that God would carry her though her dark and deep abyss of grief. Her expectant faith was not about to let her waste her pain on perpetual anger and forever asking why. Her faith resuscitated her hope when it seemed that all was hopeless. Her faith and trust in God's heavenly perspective—the big picture— pulled her through the darkness. It gave her grief meaning. It was her expectant faith that gave her strength she didn't know she had.

We can be thankful that most of us do not experience the heart-wrenching agony of burying two babies, as Nancy Guthrie did. But eventually, we each encounter a personal "faith trial"—a jolt that tests our faith at the deepest of levels. For some of us, it occurs in our careers. We lose our jobs, or our businesses fail. For others, it's a fracture in our families, whether with a rebellious child, a quarrelsome spouse, or, even worse, an act of betrayal that causes us to wonder if we even know the people we thought we knew best. Whatever the unexpected jolt may be, it's likely to be the catalyst for holding on to faith because all we have is faith— faith that spurs on hope.

WHAT CAN WE EXPECT FROM GOD?

Did you realize that knowing what to expect gives you power? It's true. Psychologists call it "cognitive control." With even a small bit of information about a situation, we feel more in control and have better outcomes than those who don't have that information.

I've long been intrigued by a simple experiment conducted in a supermarket. It focused on two groups of women. Each group was given a long shopping list. Their task was to select the best buys in the store for each item on the list. One group was told, "While you are carrying out the task, the store may become crowded. So if you feel a little anxious while you're shopping, that may be why." That was it. That's all the additional information they received. The other group of shoppers didn't get this information.

Did it make a difference? Could one little tidbit of information given to prepare for a slightly different mind-set matter? Yes, that little piece of knowledge seemed to make a big difference. The informed group got more shopping items correct, was more satisfied with the store, and felt the experience was comfortable. The uninformed group felt stressed, missed items on their lists, and didn't like the experience.[20] Having information about a situation, this study and many others have shown, frees people from "searching for explanations" and empowers them to give their attention and energy to the task.

What does this have to do with faith and hope? Quite frankly, this grocery-store scenario pales in comparison with the knowledge God wants us to have—the information he provides to give us a leg up in life. Jesus says it plainly: "Here on earth you will have many trials and sorrows."[21] You can expect it. Problems rain on all of us. Nobody gets through this life without troubles. "I have told you all this so that you may have peace in me," he says.[22] In other words, when we know what to expect, we have "cognitive control" that brings about contentment.

But take note: It's not a contentment that arrives because we got what we wished for. It's not the contentment that comes as a result of achieving a goal. It is a contentment to live with discontent until our hope is fulfilled. It is the wisdom to be content with our discontent. That's peace in spite of problems. This paradox is the only cognitive control we can claim. But it is powerful. It is strength giving.

> Everything that is done in the world is done by hope.
>
> MARTIN LUTHER KING JR.

Eugene Peterson puts it this way: "Hoping means a confident, alert expectation that God will do what he said he will do. It is imagination put in the harness of faith. It is a willingness to let God do it in his way and in his time."[23] In other words, the hope of God-followers is the opposite of making demands on God to put our plans into effect, telling him both how and when to do it. If you are placing your faith in God, the fulfillment of your hope becomes *his* agenda, not yours. You're now living by God's plan, not yours. Does this mean you merely stand passively on the sidelines? Absolutely not. You stand actively on his promises.

STANDING ON THE PROMISES

Some years ago in Rome, I had a chance to visit the catacombs, those tunnels under the ancient city where many of the early Christians were buried. If you look closely as you walk, you can see the symbols of faith on their tombs, mostly the dove, the fish, and the anchor. The dove symbolizes the Holy Spirit. The letters of the Greek word for "fish," *ichthus*, stand for the words *Jesus Christ, God's Son, Savior*. The anchor came from the idea that people of faith, especially in tough times, have hope anchored in their souls. Their hope is steadfast and secure because it is fastened on God's promises.

It should come as no surprise, really. We stake *everything* most precious in our lives on promises that have been made. And promises we expect to be kept—by our parents, our spouses, our friends. So when it comes to hoping in God's commitment to us, it is the same as any other relationship. We know that pinning our hopes on promises always comes down in the end to one thing: trust in the person who makes the promises.[24] The more we trust the promise maker, the more hope and confidence we have in the promise being kept. That's why, for people of faith, knowing God is paramount.[25] Of course, knowing God does not eliminate our doubts about God's closeness in times of trouble. Even Jesus in his desperation echoed the cry of the psalmist David: "My God, my God, why have you abandoned me?"[26]

The movie *A Beautiful Mind* tells the story of John Nash,

played by Russell Crowe, who is a brilliant mathematician struggling with mental instability. His marriage is a testimony to true commitment through years of illness and trial. On the evening he proposes, the following conversation ensues:

> Nash: "Alicia, does our relationship warrant long-term commitment? I need some kind of proof, some kind of verifiable empirical data."
> Alicia: "I'm sorry, just give me a moment to redefine my girlish notions of romance. A proof. Verifiable data. All right, how big is the universe?"
> Nash: "Infinite."
> Alicia: "How do you know?"
> Nash: "I know because all the data indicates it's infinite."
> Alicia: "But it hasn't been proven yet. You haven't seen it."
> Nash: "No."
> Alicia: "Then how do you know for sure?"
> Nash: "I don't. I just believe it."
> Alicia: "It's the same with love, I guess."[27]

It's the same for faith. You just believe. And as you believe, you come to know God. And the more you know God, the more you trust his promises—and a meaningful hope emerges.

God, as we all know, does not promise us everything we get it into our minds to hope for. But he does give us reason to believe that what he *does* promise is a commitment we can count on. One of the most emphatic statements in all of Scripture says, "I will never fail you. I will never abandon you."[28] In Greek the verse contains two double negatives, similar to saying in English, "I will never, ever, ever forsake you." Does a promise like this mean that we should feel guilty if we doubt it? No. Our doubts are just telling us that we don't know the Promise Maker well enough to trust the promise he is making. The relationship needs more time for more trust to grow.

When we put our hope in a God we cannot see or hear or touch, we are living by faith. And even faith as small as a tiny seed can do powerful things. That's why people of faith, regardless of how much faith they have, put their trust in the Maker of the universe to keep his promises.

> **Hope is faith holding out its hand in the dark.**
>
> GEORGE ILES

SEEING BEYOND THE WALLS

At the beginning of this chapter I told you about my friend Bill, who had gone to prison years before I knew him. Bill always wondered why he had stopped seeing the prison walls. Why were they there one day and gone the next—at least gone in his mind? What had changed?

In a word, faith.

In the past Bill had looked only at the obstacles. He had focused on all the limiting factors and improbable outcomes. But once he started seeing things through the lens of faith, his vision changed. Limitations, the walls in Bill's mind, weren't so big anymore when Bill started seeing the possibilities instead of the impossibilities.

This was more than a metaphor for Bill. In fact, he once told me that he can point to the place in San Quentin where he literally began seeing beyond the walls. Every day at three thirty, Bill and the other inmates filed into line in the prison yard, after just thirty minutes of breathing fresh air, to make their way back into the building and their tiny cells. The trek involved walking single file up three flights of concrete steps on the exterior of the building. These steps were more than 150 years old and solid as a rock. The side closest to the yard was lined with a half wall and a high chain-link fence. Bill walked these steps nearly every day of his prison life—always with a sense of dread and despair to be going back inside from the yard.

In fact, those steps were some of the hardest steps Bill had to take each day—not physically but mentally. And whenever he got to the top of the stairs, the landing area where a guard would eye the inmates up and down as they walked through the door, Bill would look back for a moment, almost by reflex, at the prison yard below, surrounded by the impenetrable concrete walls surrounding San Quentin.

> **The future is as bright as the promises of God.**
>
> WILLIAM CAREY

However, on one particular day, when Bill reached the top of the steps and looked back at the yard, he didn't focus so much on the yard or the walls. He saw, for the first time, really, what was beyond the walls and the chain-link fence: the beautiful green hills of Marin County. In his two and a half years in prison, Bill told me, this was the only place he ever saw beyond the physical walls of San Quentin to life on the outside.

And it was at this same time that Bill began seeing past the mental walls that were hemming him in. He began seeing that life held promise for him on the outside, but more important, on the inside, too. It did not matter whether Bill was in prison or not, he had a renewed faith in the future—Bill was thinking expectantly and finding strength in anticipation.[29]

FOR REFLECTION

1. When are you most likely to encounter "walls" in your head? What are they, and what are they preventing you from seeing? Can you recount a time when you stopped seeing particular walls?

2. Do you view yourself as a person who thinks expectantly? Are you hopeful? What are you most hopeful about, and in what areas does your hope wane? Why?

3. Do you believe in your capacity to alter your life by altering the expectations of your mind? Why or why not? And do you have a specific example from your life where your anticipations—your expectant hope—made you stronger?

4. How well do you resonate with a "hope that does not disappoint"? Most people don't know the depth of this kind of hope until they are hanging on to it through faith. Is that the case for you? How does your faith, if you have one, carry your hope? How does it sustain it?

WORKBOOK EXERCISE 2

If you are using the optional workbook, the exercise for this chapter will reveal the personal power that can be yours when you identify the places in your life where you can leverage anticipation. It will also reveal how you, with your personality, are most likely to know God and to stand on the specific promises from which you draw the most meaning and power.

MAKING IT REAL
LEVERAGING THE POWER OF YOUR MIND

The eye sees only what the mind is prepared to comprehend.

—Henri Bergson

"Knowing is not enough," said German writer Johann Wolfgang von Goethe. "We must apply!" That is so true. Knowledge without application is of little use—particularly when it comes to something as valuable as knowing how to leverage the power of your mind. So how are you doing in this area? You've read about the power of thinking simply and the power of thinking expectantly. But how does each of these often-neglected practices apply to your life?

If your dreams have been dashed by an unexpected jolt, you need the power of your mind to get you up on your feet and moving forward. You can't do that without leveraging the strength you'll find in your mind. And if your dreams have been deferred for no reason in particular, you need the power of your mind in order to reenergize your life with clarity and deeper purpose. That's the starting place for gaining renewed strength of your inactive dream.

When my friend Bill was at the top of the real-estate market in San Francisco, it never once occurred to him that he would find himself lying on the floor of a prison yard in San Quentin. Everything seemed hopeless. He literally could not get his mind clear. He felt as if he were living in a mental fog.

Do you know that feeling? Do you know how it feels to have your dreams dashed by an unexpected jolt? I can't possibly know what you are going through right now. But if your dreams have been dashed, I can tell you that you're not alone. I also know that one step toward recovery is to clear your mind. In this section, I urge you to choose one small thing out of all the suggestions I have here and commit to doing it this week. It takes only one step to begin a new path.

If, on the other hand, you've found your dreams deferred through life's inevitable pressures, I know how that happens. I've seen too many of my most talented students get distracted from their God-given dreams by opportunities that paid quick dividends but took them off the path they felt called to. I myself have felt acutely the conflicting time pressures that many of us experience in our 30s and 40s. If you have discovered your dreams deferred for way too long by distractions, you, too, need to leverage the power of your mind by clearing and focusing it. It's the starting place for renewed strength of your inactive dream, and this brief section will give you some practical ways to reclaim that dream.

ARE YOU USING THE POWER OF YOUR MIND?

A brief assessment can be like looking into a mirror. It heightens your self-awareness and can help you personalize the information you've read in the previous two chapters. So before I highlight some practical applications of the material, you may want to take a moment to complete this simple questionnaire of just ten items.

Take your time, and be honest as you consider your responses.

There are no right or wrong answers. Just answer yes, no, or maybe to each.

1. In my mind, worry often outweighs hope.

   Yes ____ No ____ Maybe ____

2. My mind often races because I have so much going on in my head.
   Yes ____ No ____ Maybe ____

3. I'm doubtful about whether the dream I have for my life will be realized.
   Yes ____ No ____ Maybe ____

4. I tend to overthink situations and problems in my life.
   Yes ____ No ____ Maybe ____

5. I sometimes doubt that I will overcome my problems.
   Yes ____ No ____ Maybe ____

6. I often get sidetracked in my thinking and struggle to stay focused.
   Yes ____ No ____ Maybe ____

7. I'm not particularly optimistic about the next few weeks.
   Yes ____ No ____ Maybe ____

8. I sometimes feel that my thinking keeps me from taking action.
   Yes ____ No ____ Maybe ____

9. I don't hear that "still, small voice" as much as I'd like to.
   Yes ____ No ____ Maybe ____

10. I tend to see more impossibilities than possibilities.
    Yes ____ No ____ Maybe ____

MAKING SENSE OF YOUR RESULTS

Give yourself 2 for every yes, 0 for every no, and 1 for every maybe. Your score will fall somewhere between 0 and 20 points.

If you scored *between 15 and 20*, you can significantly improve the power of your mind. Although you may be feeling quite powerless now, you will see dramatic advances in your sense of well-being when you apply the principles you've learned in this section of the book. There's no need to feel overwhelmed. Taking a few small action steps, noted below, will set you on the right path to leveraging the power of your mind—even if you are not optimistic.

If you scored *between 6 and 14*, you are likely to vacillate between leveraging the power of your mind and overlooking it. That is, sometimes you find great strength because you are leaning into your capacity to clear your head, and at other times, your thinking gets muddled and even obsessive. In the same way, you are sometimes at peace and hopeful about your future, but you can just as easily lose your faith in the future. You will want to pay special attention to the practical helps that follow in order to more consistently harness the power that comes from thinking simply and expectantly.

If you scored *between 0 and 5*, your mind is in prime condition to leverage the power that comes from thinking simply and thinking expectantly. Take advantage of the practical applications that follow to hone your mind's strength. In fact, you'll find a suggestion, specifically for you, for doing just that.

GETTING PERSONAL

Now that you have this bit of self-awareness in hand, I want to help you take what you have read in part 1 and apply it to the areas in your life where you will gain the greatest benefit. Because I know that every reader comes to this book with unique challenges, I encourage you to view the following suggestions as items on a menu. You'll do best if you select just two or three items that appeal to you. Don't feel that you need to take on each of them. Scan the following personal applications, and focus on the ones that pertain most to you and your situation.

LEVERAGING THE POWER OF THINKING MORE SIMPLY

In chapter 1 you saw how clearing your head helps you to discover personal strength—how it makes a way for better decisions and intuitive wisdom. Here are a few practical ways of doing just that.

◆ Get Specific

Most of us get overwhelmed when we try to apply new knowledge in every area of our lives. For this reason, I highly recommend that you begin applying this information to something specific. It may have to do with some aspect of your marriage, such as resolving conflicts with your spouse. It may have to do with a decision you're trying to make about your future or where you work. You get the idea. So, how would you complete the following sentence? The one area where I'd especially like to think more clearly in my life is _____. That's the place to begin.

Next, how do you imagine this piece of your life would be different if you could think more clearly about it? The more specifically you can see the desired result from this kind of thinking, the better.

◆ Clear Your Head

If you feel as if your mind is too often in a fog or that your thoughts are racing because you have so much going on, I encourage you to do something you probably already know to do: Write down everything that is weighing on your mind. On a sheet of paper (or a pad, if necessary), list the items that seem to be filling your head. If you are waiting for results from a medical exam, put that on the list. If it's your child's performance in an upcoming competition, write it down. Even if it's what you're having for dinner, include it. From the heavy to the frivolous, if it's in your head, put it on your list. Here's why: Research shows that this kind of "mind dump" is a surprisingly simple method for gaining almost instant clarity. As you write down these items, your mind will let many of them go so that you can give your mental attention to what matters most. Try it anytime you feel overwhelmed by what's in your mind.

◆ Breathe Easy

This suggestion is almost embarrassingly simple, but research shows it's something almost all of us need to put into practice: taking deeper breaths. It's a proven antidote to a stressed-out and racing mind. So before you brush off this suggestion as too childish or simplistic, consider the fact that most of us are unaware of our breathing patterns—especially when we're doing such common tasks as composing e-mails or sending text messages on a cell phone. When our breathing becomes shallow, insufficient fresh air reaches our lungs, and our blood is not properly purified or oxygenated. Waste products that should be removed are kept in circulation and slowly poison our systems—including our thinking (that's one of the reasons we can suffer from headaches). So here's my suggestion: Lie down on the floor, and place a book on your abdomen. Breathe deeply several times, allowing your abdomen to expand. Watch the book move up and down. Now, sit up, and try the same thing without the book. These are deep breaths. Experts suggest doing this at least three times a day.

◆ Tie Up Loose Ends

One of the most common reasons we struggle to think simply is unfinished business. Countless studies have demonstrated the negative impact an incomplete task can have on our capacity to be mentally focused. The task can be as seemingly insignificant as the need to empty the washing machine or as serious as the need to offer an apology. Unfinished business of any kind pulls us into the past and keeps us from being fully engaged in the present. What kind of unfinished business is occupying your thinking right now? And what can you do to complete the task and therefore bring closure to it? The fewer loose ends you have in your life, the more power you will find in your mind. A good place to start is to make a list of the things that seem to nag at you because they aren't done. Then resolve to check off as many of them as you can.

LEVERAGING THE POWER OF THINKING MORE EXPECTANTLY

In chapter 2 you saw how thinking expectantly helps you to find personal strength—how anticipation makes the way for hopefulness to permeate your mind. Here are a few practical ways of making this real in your own life.

◆ Counter Your Walls with Windows

If you're like most people—whether your hopes have been dashed or deferred—you have "walls" in your life. These are the barriers that only you may be seeing on your path to realizing your dreams. You may see a huge wall of hard work that seems insurmountable. Or perhaps it's a wall of criticism from others that causes you to stand still in your tracks. To leverage the power of your mind, you need to clearly identify your biggest emotional wall and counter it with a window. A "window," in this case, is a possibility, a way *through* your wall. For example, if others' criticism of you is your wall, your window may be to recognize that the criticism will be only short-term or will come from only a small group of people. The goal here is to identify as many windows in your wall as possible so that you begin to see less and less of the wall. One of the best ways to counter your walls with windows, by the way, is to examine your walls with a trusted friend who has your best interests in mind.

◆ Feed Your Faith

Lewis Smedes said that hope is made up of three ingredients: desire, belief, and worry. And, of course, it is worry that weakens hope. To counteract your worry quotient, you need to enhance your belief. In short, you need to feed your faith—and starve your worry. To do so, you may want to identify what most effectively bolsters your belief. For example, maybe it's being around other people of faith, people who infuse your own belief with confidence. Maybe it is recalling the hurdles you have already overcome to get to where you are (many people find this to offer a big boost). But refuting "irrational beliefs" can bolster nearly everyone's beliefs. Irrational beliefs are statements you frequently make to yourself that aren't backed up by evidence. Some common irrational beliefs include the following:

- I should never ask for help.
- Everyone should love me and respect what I do.
- Life should be fair.
- If I ignore the problem, it will go away.
- I should be unfailingly competent at what I undertake.
- I'm helpless.

The more you dwell on an irrational belief, the more likely you are to worry. So what's the solution? First, identify your irrational self-talk. Then refute it by asking yourself to find any rational support for the statement. If you tell yourself that you're helpless, for example, ask yourself, *What evidence is there to support my belief?* You will likely be forced to conclude that there is no evidence. None. Therefore, you are *not* a helpless person. Now, find an alternative statement to your irrational self-talk. Say instead, "I may *feel* helpless, but I'm not." Doing this kind of exercise consistently will feed your faith and, in turn, heighten your hope.

◆ Inventory Your Hopes

One of the best ways to leverage the strength that comes from thinking expectantly is to take inventory of what you are hoping for. Have you ever made a list of your top ten hopes—the things you are hoping for most right now? I encourage you to make such a list, because doing so will help you measure how meaningful your individual hopes are. For example, among your top ten hopes you might say you're hoping your child gets into a good college. You're hoping a friend is healed of cancer. You're hoping you get a raise. You'll have no trouble coming up with ten; the challenge will be limiting your list to just that many. Once you've done this, I recommend that you measure the depth of your hopes by ordering them from the deepest and most meaningful to you to the most shallow and least meaningful. This will cause you to carefully consider each of your top ten hopes. The deeper your hopes, as I said in chapter 2, the more satisfying your life will be. Next, I recommend that you note one or two tangible steps you can take this week to get you closer to realizing each of your hopes. By the way, this is not a onetime exercise. You can inventory your hopes time and time again. A monthly or quarterly "hope inventory" will keep you thinking expectantly about the things that matter most—especially when you add tangible steps toward seeing those hopes become realities.

◆ *Focus on the Big Picture*

If you're like most people, you likely lose the strength that can be found in anticipation because life's inevitable inconveniences distract you from what really matters. A family member who makes a mess or even a total stranger who causes you irritation can distract you from what really matters. That's only human, of course. It's easy to get derailed by little irritants that keep you from being the kind of person you want to be. But you can get back on track by regaining your view of the big picture and, thus, diminish the emotional impact of something that bothers you. You do this by catching even a little glimpse of the "eternal perspective"— as cliché as that may sound—and by asking a single question: What really matters in this moment? If you can gather your wits about you and pose that question to yourself, you will see that a mess on the kitchen floor matters far less than children's need to know that you love them even when they do make a mess.

PART 2
THE POWER OF YOUR HEART

Once I had brains and a heart also;
so, having tried them both, I should much rather
have a heart.

—TIN WOODMAN IN *The Wonderful*
Wizard of Oz

Every day, a ten-ounce muscle—the most powerful muscle in our body—contracts one hundred thousand times and rarely misses a beat. After all, the cardiovascular system, commanded by the heart, is unforgiving of errors. Over a lifetime, the two high-capacity pumps in the heart beat 2.5 billion times and pump sixty million gallons of blood without pausing to rest.[1] *Remarkable.*

Yet the human heart is more than the commander of the circulatory system. These days, few people view the heart only as a blood-pumping station. Scientists know that the heart is an emotional organ and that it has a relationship with the "emotional brain." Some researchers are even asking whether, in addition to being emotional, the heart could also be an organ of intelligence that works in unison with the brain.[2]

According to a study published in the *New England Journal of Medicine*, memory, attention, and concentration somewhat declined immediately after coronary bypass surgery, and similar declines were observed five years after. The heart physically communicates with the brain and the rest of the body. The communication pathways, which originate in the heart, travel through the emotional memory section of the brain and go to areas responsible for reasoning. The pulse created by the heart is actually like a "blood pressure wave" that reaches and energizes every cell of the body and brain.[3]

As a psychologist, I have sometimes helped people manage their stress through "biofeedback," a process that measures indicators such as skin temperature, muscle tension, and heart rate and then conveys them back to patients in real time (usually through a tone). The tone raises patients' awareness of their bodies and, therefore, the possibility of conscious control. One thing that often surprises me is how in-control, strong, and stoic some people can appear to be, yet when we measure blood pressure and heart rate, it becomes painfully obvious how much they are masking their true tensions and troubles. My job is to help them get in touch with their insides—their hearts—both literally and figuratively. They need to see how their troubled and racing hearts are revealing their troubled and insecure feelings.

This is why expressions such as "My heart aches," "Open your heart," or "My heart goes out to you" are often more than symbolic.[4] They make a deeper connection than mere rational thought. They resonate in the heart of human emotion. How do we know? We know it in our hearts. According to folk wisdom, the heart is the seat of emotion, love, creativity, gratitude, and so on. The finest of human values rest within our hearts.

Intelligence alone, without involvement of the heart, can be dangerous.[5] We run the risk of becoming "heartless." Or having a heart of stone. It's what Antoine de Saint-Exupéry was getting at when he said, "The eyes are blind. One must look with the heart." Jesus highlighted the importance of the heart when he said, "Out of the overflow of the heart the mouth speaks."[6] Without the heart, we lack emotional sensitivity and understanding. Without the heart, we lack a major component of human strength.

FEEL VULNERABLE AND FEEL CONNECTED

The two chapters in this section will show you how to find power in your heart—how to feel with strength.

Chapter 3, "Feel Vulnerable," reveals the power of a great paradox: When we admit our weakness, we find our strength. It's strange, but true. We want to *be* strong, so we try to *appear* strong— even to ourselves. We keep a stiff upper lip and stay tough. But we neglect the fact that vulnerability slays our weakness. And when we conceal our vulnerability, our pain, embarrassment, and weakness grow. The solution is to admit our vulnerability—to ourselves. That's easier said than done, of course. In our look-at-me culture, admitting weakness feels like swimming against a powerful riptide. But the effort is worth it, for once we own our weakness, once we confess the fact that we need help, that we are sometimes powerless, we step over unhealthy pride and become authentic. And that's where much of the power of our hearts resides, in being real, because our hearts are where genuine love is felt.

Chapter 4, "Feel Connected," takes your self-awareness to the next level. While the previous chapter is about connecting with ourselves, this chapter is about connecting with others. We all live in a web of social connection. But many of us find it difficult to make ourselves known—*really known*—to the people in our lives. In fact, most of us, even with close relationships, don't leverage the power those relationships can instill in our hearts. We harbor secrets. We wear masks that make us appear stronger than we really are. And if we feel that others could never understand our pain because they haven't suffered it, we keep them at arm's length with flimsy, prideful attitudes that say our pain makes us impossible to know.

YOUR HEART IS STRONGER THAN YOU KNOW

At just twenty-four years of age, an expectant mother faced an unthinkable decision, a choice no one should ever have to make. When she was diagnosed with a malignant brain tumor, she had to decide whether to undergo treatment for her cancer, which would likely kill the baby, or risk her own life and wait to begin treatment until the baby could live on her own.

In a stunning act of heartfelt devotion to her baby, the woman chose to delay treatment until she knew the baby was strong enough to survive on her own. Linda Chassiakos, a pediatrician involved in the case, recounted the harrowing tale to the *Los Angeles Times*: "Doctors told the mother that if she didn't treat the aggressive tumor immediately, she would likely die. But the fetus would probably not survive treatment." The expectant mother, wanting to protect her unborn child, decided to delay treatment for herself. Within days she slipped into a coma.

"To our astonishment—and joy—the comatose woman 'hung in' until the 28th week," said Dr. Chassiakos. "At that point, an ultrasound showed the fetus was probably over the 2-pound mark, and her doctors scheduled the caesarean. Gasping for air, the child was born at a size and weight that would give her a fighting chance of life."[7]

The mother's surgery followed, and doctors removed enough of the tumor so she could regain consciousness and meet her tiny daughter. Although the baby developed lung and gastrointestinal infections, her long-term prognosis was good. The mother, however, was not so fortunate. Two weeks before the baby was released from the hospital, her mother died.

We can be thankful that most of us will never face such a terrible ordeal. But such a story still causes us to ask, Where does anyone get the strength to face such a horrific decision? Where does one find the bravery? In this case, most would say it came straight from that mother's heart. Some may even argue that only a mother's heart could make such a sacrificial choice. Maybe. But as you will see in chapters 3 and 4, all of us, mothers or not, have reservoirs of strength and power in our hearts to face any number of hurdles and hardships—if we know where to find them.

3

FEEL VULNERABLE
THERE'S STRENGTH
IN OWNING YOUR
WEAKNESS

Weakness is nourished by concealment.
—Latin Proverb

I have always been a man with a plan. Even as a kid, I knew how to delay gratification and set goals for the future. I saved my money from an early age and even bought my first share of AT&T stock as a sixth grader with lunch money I had saved. I wasn't bossy or domineering, but I *was* driven. A type A personality from the start.

This means that, for good or ill, I live with a sense of urgency. If there's a deadline, I like to meet it—ahead of time. I keep my to-do list short. I plan my work and work my plan, as the productivity gurus say. My plan after college was to marry the girl I had dated since we were teenagers. And I did. After graduating from college, we headed for Los Angeles and graduate school. I planned to earn two degrees in six years, and I did. Check, check.

I'm not saying that everything came easily. My plan required a lot of effort and willpower. I frequently had to maneuver around obstacles and adjust my efforts. But I generally kept moving forward, even when it got tough. I'd study harder, stay up later, forgo rewards—whatever it took.

From graduate school it was on to a competitive fellowship in medical psychology at the University of Washington in Seattle. Why? Because it was part of the plan. I wanted to teach at Seattle Pacific University across town, and I knew the fellowship would set me up for that position. I didn't apply anywhere else, and a year later I got the job. Check.

> How often it is that the angry man rages denial of what his inner self is telling him.
>
> FRANK HERBERT

A few more goals lay on the immediate horizon: climb the academic ranks toward full professorship, buy our first home, and write a few books. Check, check, and check again.

Everything was going according to plan—until we had our first baby. Complications that were not entirely clear led the doctor to put my wife, Leslie, on round-the-clock bed rest just three months into the pregnancy. She was to remain on her left side as much as possible and could leave the house only for medical appointments. With each visit to the doctor, we received increasingly bad news. The status of the baby and of Leslie's own health was in jeopardy.

Because the doctor said the possibility of our baby's surviving would be slim, we decided not to decorate a nursery.

"I'm not sure what's happening," the doctor told us, "but from the sonogram we can see that your baby isn't getting the nutrition he needs. He's not growing." That's when he admitted Leslie into the hospital, six months into the pregnancy.

With my wife's life at serious risk, our baby boy, John, was born two weeks later on February 8, in an emergency delivery.

He was three months premature and weighed just over a pound. Doctors rushed him into the Neonatal Intensive Care Unit (NICU), where they connected him to monitors and to machines that helped him breathe, regulated his temperature, and did everything else a tiny body needs in order to live.

I've got to admit that at that point I felt just as vulnerable as he was. My well-ordered life was far beyond my control. Seeing my wife so ill and the tiny frame of my son, barely hanging on to life, was almost more than I could bear. We didn't know if John would make it, and more than one doctor suggested we prepare for the worst. But John made it through his first night. And his second.

A week went by, and then I was awakened out of a restless sleep by a phone call from the primary nurse, who told me that my baby boy was going into emergency surgery. I raced to the hospital and arrived just in time to see his one-pound body being wheeled down the corridor on an adult-size gurney surrounded by two surgeons and four technicians.

I could barely stand. I felt as if I couldn't breathe.

This surgery was a devastating blow. John was already fighting for his life in the NICU, and we felt this news could be signaling the beginning of the end. We were heavy with sadness and eerily silent. Since I had spent much of my graduate and postgraduate training in hospital and surgical settings, I begged to observe the surgery but was refused. All we could do was wait.

> **If we refuse to take the risk of being vulnerable, we are already half-dead.**
>
> MADELEINE L'ENGLE

The procedure lasted nearly three hours, but it seemed like three days. Finally the chief surgeon walked into the waiting room and sat on the coffee table in front of us to give us the news. His face gave no clue as to the condition of our child. Leslie was holding my hand so tightly that I'm surprised she didn't sprain it as we heard the surgeon say that baby John's abdominal surgery had been successful.

For the next three months, John lay in his Isolette in the NICU. And every day we sat by his side in our sterile gowns as the machines around him hummed, whirred, and beeped.

After more surgeries, John, by now weighing just over three pounds and tethered to a six-foot oxygen tank, finally came home—the smallest baby ever to be released from Swedish Hospital in Seattle. But we weren't home free. The months ahead would include frantic 911 calls, sleepless nights, and for me, feeling desperately out of control. All my well-laid plans and goals had jumped the rails. Life was careening out of control, and I felt helpless. I couldn't do anything more to aid my fragile son. We were in a broken place, and I, so used to being in control, couldn't fix it. My heart was weak. I had never felt more powerless. Never more vulnerable.

But I didn't want to admit it. Who does? The very idea of confessing our weakness when we need to be strong goes against our grain, whether we're control freaks or not. Vulnerability is not an experience we humans readily embrace. We would rather deny the fact that we're feeling needy, unprotected, and exposed. But as you're about to see, we do so at our peril.

That's why I dedicate this chapter to the benefit that can come from feeling vulnerable. I want to help you to find strength in owning your weakness.

IGNORING YOUR WEAKNESS MAKES YOU WEAK

Over two million people gather for meetings every day. Almost around the clock, there is a meeting starting in an hour at a location fairly close to you. There are no dues, no budgets, no buildings. Attendance is free—as long as you admit your weakness.

In June 1935, Bill Wilson, a stockbroker suffering from

an uncontrollable drinking problem, started the first Alcoholics Anonymous (AA) group in Akron, Ohio, when he met Robert Holbrook Smith, a surgeon, a total stranger, and also an alcoholic. Today, AA groups number more than one hundred thousand and meet in 150 countries. Millions upon millions have found healing and meaning as a result of these meetings. Millions upon millions have found strength to overcome what had rendered them helpless.

And for each one, that healing starts with a single step: admitting that they are powerless.

Why would this be the starting place? After all, the goal is to gain power and strength over a demon that has knocked you off your feet. So why start by admitting your weakness?

On the surface, it doesn't make sense. It's illogical. A contradiction. One of life's ultimate paradoxes. Yet this seeming impossibility is the great untapped reservoir of strength within the human heart. Contemporary stud-

> **God has given you one face, and you make yourself another.**
>
> WILLIAM SHAKESPEARE

ies have borne this out time and again. There is strength in owning our weakness—admitting to ourselves that we need help, that we can't make it on our own, and that we still have interior work to do. And when we conceal our weakness, when we attempt to keep it hidden even from ourselves, we only compound the problem.

For more than two decades, Northeastern University's Randall Colvin conducted a study that underscores how important it is to have a sense of one's own weakness.[1] He and his team tracked 130 individuals from nursery school, checking in with them at various points into their twenties. They monitored such things as the subjects' dependability and how well they handled life's frustrations. The volunteers provided self-descriptions, and their friends contributed evaluations as well.

The researchers found that some of the subjects' personalities did not line up well with their self-images. Some of them had a tough time admitting they didn't have it all together. In other words, who they were in reality and how they *perceived* themselves were out of alignment. And when that was the case, an unfortunate portrait emerged.

"These subjects tend to lack social skills, and appear anxious and moody," says Colvin. "They are sensitive to criticism and sometimes keep people at a distance without knowing it—perhaps so that they don't get negative feedback that might alter their self-perception. They are trying to hide their flaws from themselves."[2]

> An anxious heart weighs a man down.
>
> PROVERBS 12:25 (MHJ)

Although these individuals may have been deluding themselves, they were not fooling their friends. Even their pals described them as somewhat condescending. And when friends saw through the facade, the subjects engaged in even more distortion and denial in an attempt to maintain a positive self-view. Their friends didn't see them as authentic or genuine. They saw them as people who weren't comfortable in their own skins. The subjects want to feel good about themselves. They want to be secure and strong. But inside, even when they are unwilling to admit it, they are broken. They feel desperately insecure. In other words, they haven't yet come to own their weakness.

All this suggests that artificially propping up our self-esteem by not admitting our weakness may provide a temporary mental boost, but in the long run, doing so stunts our social and personal well-being.[3] In other words, not admitting our weakness makes us weak.

BUT WHAT ABOUT "I ♥ ME"?

It's easy to see why so many of us have a tough time owning our weaknesses. Our culture propagates self-appreciation that borders on delusion.[4] A popular poster proclaims, "The most important thing is how you see yourself," above a picture of a tabby kitten looking in the mirror and seeing a large lion. The message: See yourself as much better—and much stronger—than you actually are. Popular self-help author Wayne Dyer takes this concept to a whole new level: "The best thing about Jesus was that he had a mom that believed he was the son of God," he says. "Imagine how much better the world would be if all of our moms thought that way."[5] Apparently Dyer believes that we should all be raised to believe that we are God's greatest gift to humanity.

"Loving yourself means knowing how great you are and not letting any person, any place, or any thing ever get in the way of that," writes Diane Mastromarino in her aptly titled book *The Girl's Guide to Loving Yourself: A Book about Falling in Love with the One Person Who Matters Most . . . You.*[6] I'm not pointing to just a handful of voices proclaiming this message of self-admiration. These are a small sample of the hundreds of thousands of tips for "loving yourself." If you don't believe me, just do a quick online search of the topic. There you'll find innumerable helps, everything from audio recordings for "soaring self-esteem" to "self-affirmation cards" to T-shirts that say "I ♥ ME." Self-esteem is considered, as one author put it, our "national wonder drug."[7]

Let's be clear. I have no beef with the idea of self-esteem. Not at all. In fact, a healthy self-image is essential to our dignity. Self-acceptance enables us to love other people with the best of motives. Without a balanced sense of self-worth and inner security, it's impossible to cultivate character qualities such as humility and empathy. But too often in our current culture, healthy self-esteem is mistaken for vanity. It's mistaken for an intolerance of self-perceived weakness that can border on narcissism.[8]

> **Growth begins when we begin to accept our own weakness.**
>
> JEAN VANIER

Here is my point: When it comes to owning our weakness, we are going against the current of our narcissistic culture. To admit, simply to ourselves, that we have a flaw, a failing, or a limitation is to break the code of self-admiration. If you bristle at the notion of this chapter, that may be why.

Of course, you may not resist the thought of owning your weakness at all. Maybe your weakness is all you tend to see. You feel vulnerable—open to being wounded—on a daily basis. Think, for example, of a woman who, in spite of doing everything humanly possible to rear a responsible son, has watched that young man go off the deep end and throw off everything he used to value. Those who have watched her perseverance over the years in the face of this daunting challenge and heartache are drawn to her, but she feels she has nothing to offer them because her apparent "failure" as a parent is on display every time her son gets into trouble again. Like this woman, you may struggle with owning your strength. And that, as we'll see, is *your* weakness.

> God allows us to experience the low points of life in order to teach us lessons we could not learn in any other way. The way we learn those lessons is not to deny the feelings but to find the meanings underlying them.
>
> STANLEY LINDQUIST

YOU'RE ABOVE AVERAGE, AREN'T YOU?

Because of our cultural leanings toward unbridled self-admiration, you may be tempted to believe that owning your weakness is a call to humility or meekness. And you'd be right. But before you write this off as a slap in the face of your self-esteem, consider what it means to be meek.

It doesn't mean to be cowardly or spineless. "The meek man is not a human mouse afflicted with a sense of his own inferiority," said A. W. Tozer. "Rather, he may be in his moral life as bold as a lion and as strong as Samson; but he has stopped being fooled about himself." That's the key. To not be fooled by ourselves. That's what owning our weakness is all about.

If you're thinking that you're not like other people—that you're not likely to be fooled by self-deception, think again. None of us are beyond deceiving ourselves.[9] Psychologists David Dunning and Justin Kruger tested students at Cornell University on a range of subjects from logical reasoning to grammar to the ability to spot a funny joke. They compared how well people thought they did with how well they actually did. "Overall, people overestimated themselves," said Dunning. "And those who did worst were most likely to think they had outperformed everyone else. Incompetent people don't know they're incompetent."[10]

We all dismiss certain facts as incompatible with how we want to see ourselves. We exchange certain weaknesses in favor of other, less threatening and more agreeable ones. We twist the truth without any awareness that we are doing so. Consider the findings of a few sample studies:

- Ninety-four percent of university professors think they are better at their jobs than their colleagues.
- Seventy percent of college students think they are above average in leadership ability. Only 2 percent think they are below average.
- Eighty-five percent of medical students think it is improper for politicians to accept gifts from lobbyists. Only 46 percent think it's improper for physicians to accept gifts from drug companies.
- A study of medical residents found that 84 percent thought their colleagues were influenced by gifts from pharmaceutical companies, but only 16 percent thought that they were similarly influenced.[11]

Without flinching, almost all of us see ourselves above the midline on many of our self-perceptions. It's a psychological fact.[12] I demonstrate it every autumn in one of my entry-level psychology courses at the university. I administer a simple survey to my two hundred students in which they end up ranking their own interpersonal abilities compared with those of other students on campus. In other words, they are ranking, relative to their peers, how well they get along with others. I collect the information, tabulate the results, and display it on the screen. The results are predictable. All of the students, every single one, see themselves as "above average." They can't help but laugh out loud as they see the results. "Isn't it amazing," I say, tongue in cheek, "that in this class of two hundred students we lucked out in having *everyone* above average?" They laugh some more.

> God loves us the way we are, but too much to leave us that way.
>
> LEIGHTON FORD

Then I reveal on the screen another tidbit from the survey: An astounding 25 percent see themselves in the top one percent in terms of their ability to get along with others. This time, the students don't laugh—they gasp.

Some of us are apparently far above average, with a surprising number of people joining us.

HAVE YOU BOUGHT THE LIE?

How is it that fifty students out of two hundred see themselves in the upper echelons of interpersonal savvy? Simply because it's more satisfying to believe good things about oneself than to face the truth. In these situations, life cuts us a deal: Believe the truth, or deceive yourself. Generally speaking, we go with the latter. It rubs us the wrong way to admit—even to ourselves—our weakness, even if that "weakness" is not being better than others. This doesn't mean we're sociopathic or narcissistic. It means we're human. It's our nature to dismiss certain facts that are incompatible with our self-image. We all do it without a second thought.

Of course, self-deception doesn't always work. Sometimes we are flat out forced to see that we failed. We can't deny failing an exam or the fact that we ran our car into a mailbox. That's when we try to rationalize our behavior: "I didn't have time to study" or "My spouse messed with the rearview mirror." Or we may rationalize without even first making an effort not to: "I *need* to lie on these financial forms so that I can feed my family." Sometimes we avoid a difficult decision altogether by rationalizing our procrastination: "Sure, I'll contribute to your cause, but only after I check with my spouse, accountant, and bank."

We may frequently avoid telling ourselves the truth, but that's not always bad.[13] "Truths and roses have thorns about them," said Thoreau. The truth can hurt, and it can take

> **Our strength grows out of our weakness.**
>
> RALPH WALDO EMERSON

time to see it clearly. That's the point: The abilities that contribute to self-deception are not necessarily wrong in themselves. We go wrong with them when we routinely use self-deception to convince ourselves that we are better than we actually are. That's when we buy the lie that says, "If I'm not so bad, I don't have to change."

That little nugget, fueled by our pride, lasts only so long. We can't hold on to it indefinitely if we want to find true strength. Sooner or later, we have to examine our lives, face the truth, and become the people we were meant to be.

THE UNEXAMINED LIFE

Few would dispute the enormous impact of the Greek philosopher Plato. He touched on virtually every problem explored by subsequent philosophers. His works are counted among the world's finest literature. And if you were to ask anyone "in the know" to quote him, more often than not you would hear a simple sentence that has become his trademark: "The unexamined life is not worth living."

Those of every generation must learn to examine their lives, to make their unconscious more conscious, to diminish their blind spots, and to expose their vulnerabilities in order to become congruent, that is, to become whole and healthy.

It all hinges on awareness. You can't change what you do not acknowledge. Fyodor Dostoyevsky said, "There are things which a man is afraid to tell even to himself, and every decent man has a number of such things stored away in his mind." He was talking about examining our lives, looking into our hearts, and owning our weakness.

> The trouble with steeling yourself against the harshness of reality is that the same steel that secures your life against being destroyed secures your life also against being opened up and transformed by the holy power that life itself comes from.
>
> FREDERICK BUECHNER

AWARENESS IS CURATIVE

Self-awareness gives us the capacity to face and accept what we tend to deny.[14] When we examine our own lives and become more attentive to what's going on within our hearts, life becomes more clear. Self-awareness helps us align ourselves with the lives we want to live. Self-awareness moderates our interior world.[15] Our emotions are an easy example. That's part of the driving force behind Daniel Goleman's bestselling book *Emotional Intelligence: Why It Can Matter More Than IQ*.[16] We become smarter and stronger when we can simply identify what we are feeling. Our heavy hearts become less heavy when we articulate our emotions.

Research reveals that people who are exposed to terrible

accidents often repair unsettling scenes in their memory. But if they have help in identifying their own feelings about witnessing the accident, if they become more aware of their emotional terrain, their feeling of distress dissipates much more quickly.[17]

Another study focused on people who were laid off and were understandably angry. Researchers had half of them keep a journal for five days, spending just twenty minutes writing out their deepest feelings (a common exercise in raising self-awareness). Did it make a difference? Those who kept journals found new jobs faster than those who didn't.[18] Their heightened self-awareness alleviated their anger, lowered their stress, and enabled them to become productive more quickly.

In neither of these experiments did the subjects' emotions need to be expressed to someone else. It was enough for the individuals simply to be aware of their feelings. They needed to articulate them to themselves. That's emotional clarity. And dozens of studies have shown that it helps us manage our bad moods and soothe our frustrations or calm our annoyances. In short, self-awareness lowers our stress.

> **The first step to improvement, whether mental, moral, or religious, is to know ourselves—our weakness, errors, deficiencies, and sins.**
>
> TYRONE EDWARDS

Without self-awareness, we are surprisingly oblivious to stress. We allow it to quietly creep in and dismantle our contentment. We let stress sabotage our efforts and elongate our suffering. But once we diminish our blind spots, stress fades more quickly and keeps its distance more often.

Emotional clarity is only one example of self-awareness. The benefits of avoiding an unexamined life go much deeper, particularly when it comes to identifying, articulating, and owning our deepest weakness.

OUR DEEPEST WEAKNESS

The passenger liner *Titanic* was spared no expense to make sure it would be unsinkable. "Not even God could sink the *Titanic*" was the boast of those who put their confidence in the vessel. The ship's officers didn't even bother to get accurate information on possible hazards that might lie in its course. The luxury ship had two lookouts on its masts, but no one saw the need to place binoculars there. The crew couldn't see far enough ahead to react to danger, and they had no way to get their information to the captain if they *did* see a problem ahead.

> Most of the trouble in the world is caused by people wanting to be important.
>
> T. S. ELIOT

We all know what happened. In April 1912, the "unsinkable" ocean liner, sailing from Southampton, England, to New York, collided with an iceberg and went to its death, along with most of its passengers. As the proverb says, "Pride goes before destructon."[19]

And isn't it true? Our self-confidence can sometimes get the better of us. When we put our full weight behind our own judgment, ability, or power, we inevitably push humility out of our hearts. Self-satisfaction and unhealthy pride become visible on the surface, but their danger is submerged in our unconscious. All the while, we begin to feel pretty good about ourselves, as if we actually are better than others.

I want to make this clear: Healthy pride, the pleasant emotion of being pleased by our work, is quite different from unhealthy pridefulness, in which our egos are bloated.[20] The latter is laced with arrogance and conceit. And that's what, in this chapter, I am calling our deepest weakness. Why? Because it leads to wayward hearts. We don't have to be egomaniacs to suffer from unhealthy pride. It has a way of secretly seeping into the crevices of our lives even when we are consciously inclined to avoid it. Ironically, our very efforts to be humble can be tinged with a tendency to look down on other people who, we believe, are not.[21] It's what C. S. Lewis was getting at: "A man is never so proud as when striking an attitude of humility."[22]

Jesus used a story to demonstrate the irony of pride and humility in our lives—especially in our relationship with God. He told the story to people who were particularly pleased with themselves:

> *Two men went up to the Temple to pray, one a Pharisee, the other a tax man. The Pharisee posed and prayed like this: "Oh, God, I thank you that I am not like other people— robbers, crooks, adulterers, or, heaven forbid, like this tax man. I fast twice a week and tithe on all my income."*
>
> *Meanwhile the tax man, slumped in the shadows, his face in his hands, not daring to look up, said, "God, give mercy. Forgive me, a sinner."*
>
> *Jesus commented, "This tax man, not the other, went home made right with God. If you walk around with your nose in the air, you're going to end up flat on your face, but if you're content to be simply yourself, you will become more than yourself."*[23]

Unhealthy pride, even for sincere God-followers, is a prevalent problem. We all struggle to strike a balance between healthy pride and healthy humility. And it becomes a surreptitious problem whenever we allow it to stand in the way of opportunities to tap into God's power. That's why we call it our greatest weakness.[24] Pride prevents us from owning our neediness. It wants to focus attention on anything else but that. Pride flourishes in the dark corners of our hearts, the most self-centered places, where we want to prove our independence. In the end, pride prevents us from owning our weakness and, in turn, proves little more than how much we need God's strength.

TOO MUCH OF A GOOD THING?

The antidote to unhealthy pride is, of course, humility. And the word from which we get *humility* literally means "from the earth." In other words, humility steps off its high horse to be common and lowly.

In Nikos Kazantzakis's novel *Christ Recrucified*, there is a scene in which four village men confess their sins to one another in the presence of the pope. One of the men, Michelis, cries out in bloated humility, "How can God let us live on the earth? Why doesn't he kill us to purify creation?"

"Because, Michelis," the pope answers, "God is a potter; he works in mud."[25]

Whether you see it the same way or not, the point is that humility is lowly. And that's where God meets us—in the places in which we are humble. That's where we become malleable. Humility is the opposite of pride. Pride is riddled with self-doubt that's desperate to deny any weakness. So it swings the heart's pendulum of self-assessment toward feelings of superiority. Humility does the opposite. Well, not exactly, because healthy humility is not about feeling inferior. In fact, there are actually two kinds of humility.

> The greatest of faults, I should say, is to be conscious of none.
>
> THOMAS CARLYLE

Two Kinds of Humility

True humility is grounded in a sense of dignity and self-worth. In other words, it seeks an accurate inventory of both strengths and weaknesses. When it receives a compliment, it doesn't deflect it with self-effacement and demure posturing. That's the approach of false humility, which is built on self-depreciation. False humility clumsily dismisses its own gifts, talents, and accomplishments out of hand. "Oh, I had nothing to do with it," false humility says in response to someone's compliment for hard work.

False humility's self-appraisal is just as unhelpful and distorted as pride's. While pride takes the position of superiority, false humility takes the position of inferiority. Both are unrealistic, and neither is healthy.

The goal is to have a truly humble heart that recognizes positive attributes as well as inadequacies. It's a heart that shines a light into its dark corners and confesses its neediness.

THE HUMBLE HEART

Maybe you've seen the bumper sticker that says, "The person who can smile when things are going badly has just thought of someone to blame it on." It's a sad fact that this is sometimes not too far from the truth. We humans abhor vulnerability. And nothing makes us feel more vulnerable than admitting our imperfections and confessing our true neediness. We'd much rather find someone or something else to blame.

Better yet, we'd like to guard against the need for vulnerability by being blameless ourselves. What could guarantee emotional invulnerability more than doing everything right? When our hearts are puffed with pride, we strive for perfection so that we will be loved and admired. If we can only manage to be perfect, we'll be blameless. Everyone, even God, will have to love us. Admitting any weakness, any mistake, we think, makes us vulnerable to rejection.

And it does. When we take off our protective armor in the name of honest self-disclosure, someone may take advantage of us. It's the way of the world. But with God, there is a twist. And it always works in our favor. Our vulnerability draws God to us.

Our helplessness reveals his presence. Our weakness makes known his strength. And our confessions prompt his grace.

The message of this chapter hangs on the hinge of God's grace. Why? Because God says, "My grace is all you need. My power works best in weakness."[26] That's the paradox. Because of God's grace, we find strength in owning our weakness. God-followers can live in reckless abandon with their weakness before God. We have no need to disguise our vulnerabilities. No need for prideful pretenses of perfection.

> Oh, that God the gift would give us to see ourselves as others see us.
>
> ROBERT BURNS

The more we own our weakness, the more we experience God's grace. The Bible echoes this truth again and again: "God goes against the willful proud; God gives grace to the willing humble."[27]

That's a tough pill to swallow.

Powerless. That single word stops many people dead in their tracks. It's the biggest hurdle for most potential AA members because it's the first step in the list of the well-known Twelve Steps. Newcomers are either insulted because the first step wounds their pride, or they decide, "If that's the case, then nothing I do matters, so why try?" But a seasoned AA member will tell you that the first step doesn't mean much without the next two: believing in a Power greater than yourself and making a decision to turn your will over to the care of God. The same is true for all of us. Willpower is not enough. We need God's power. And we find it only when we set aside our pride and acknowledge we aren't God.

"The only thing I need to know about God," says the common AA slogan, "is that I ain't Him." It's undoubtedly simplistic, but in its own humble way, it makes a cogent point. We are not God. What a relief!

When I held my three-pound baby boy with a surgical scar running the full length of his abdomen, I never felt weaker. I gathered every ounce of strength I could muster to make it through that frightful season. But it wasn't enough. My back literally seized up from bearing a burden I couldn't control. My personal resources were spent. I finally came to a place, literally, at the side of a road outside the doors of the hospital, where I confessed that I wasn't God—that I couldn't make it on my own.

In a sense, I was shining a light on the pride that was holding tight to the dark corners of my heart. In all humility, I asked God to carry the burden that was breaking my back. I asked God to carry me, my wife, and our baby. And, by his grace, he did. I didn't have to earn it. And I certainly didn't have to be blameless or perfect. But I can tell you this: When I owned my weakness, God's power was made perfect.

> **Give all your worries and cares to God, for he cares about you.**
> 1 PETER 5:7

These days, that baby boy is twelve years old. Aside from the scars he wears under his shirt, you'd never know he'd had such a tough start. This child is a blessing beyond measure to us. He's a gift of grace Leslie and I never take for granted. But I have got to be honest: Pride still finds a way into my heart. As life has moved along, my hard-driving plans and goals rarely place humility on my daily agenda. But in my more enlightened moments, I send pride packing by confessing that I still can't make it on my own. I need God because I'm not a perfect friend, I'm not a perfect colleague, I'm not a perfect parent, and I'm not a perfect husband. Most of all, I need God because I'm not a perfect God-follower. My pride can sabotage my best intentions. I don't have what it takes. I can will it, but I don't do it.[28] I confess it: I need help.

And in those moments, I am strong.

FOR REFLECTION

1. How do you instinctively react to the idea of feeling vulnerable? What, in specific terms, makes you feel most emotionally insecure with yourself?

2. When you examine your life, as Plato suggests, what do you feel needs the most attention? About what areas would you like to have more self-awareness, and why? What would that awareness do for you?

3. Do you agree that your greatest weakness is pride? Why or why not? What is a specific situation in which your pride got the better of you?

4. When are you least inclined to confess your need of God, and when are you most inclined to confess your need of God? Why? Do you find that the latter gives you emotional strength? If so, how?

WORKBOOK EXERCISE 3

If you are using the optional workbook, the exercise for this chapter will help you to identify the places in your own heart where unhealthy pride seems most prevalent. It will also reveal to what degree your personality is inclined toward false humility. Finally, the exercise will give you a clear picture of the personal power that can be yours when you own your weakness.

4

FEEL CONNECTED
THERE'S STRENGTH
IN BEING KNOWN

*If you want to go fast, go alone. If you want
to go far, go together.*
—African Proverb

I n 1934, Rear Admiral Richard Byrd spent five winter months
alone, living in a feeble shelter on the Ross Ice Barrier near
the South Pole and enduring the "coldest cold on the face of the
earth."[1] The terrain was a sheet of ice thousands of feet thick,
with mountains of powdery snow shifting across its threatening
surface. The temperature often dropped to eighty below zero. In
mid-April the sun dipped below the horizon and didn't return for
weeks, a time Byrd described as "one layer of darkness piled on top
of the other."[2] In addition, the honored explorer suffered frostbite,
carbon monoxide poisoning, disturbed sleep, and malnutrition.

When Admiral Byrd returned to civilization and wrote an
account of his exploration, the title of his book did not emphasize
the terrain, the weather, the danger, the darkness, or the sickness.
A single word underscored the horror of being isolated from other
people—*Alone.*[3]

Those who are hiding their weakness, their pain, their flaws, or their failings can identify with that solitary title. We don't have to suffer the cold of the Antarctic to feel alone. The bone-cutting chill of nearly any relationship in which we are not known for who we really are will bring about an eerie sense of isolation.

Even if we are surrounded by numerous loved ones who want to be supportive, our emotional isolation can be frightfully numbing.[4] Personal pain and feelings of inadequacy separate us from the pack. In fact, MRIs show that the same region of the brain is activated whether we are feeling the pain of aloneness or physical pain.[5] It is a deeply disruptive hurt. We are hardwired for connection with one another. Our social environment affects the neural and hormonal signals that govern our attitudes and behaviors. Loneliness, for example, actually has the power to alter our immune systems.[6] Our need for social support is deeply woven into who we are as human beings.[7]

National surveys, in fact, find that a quarter of all Americans say they've felt lonely in the last month.[8] And two-thirds of Americans who don't confess to feeling lonely say that having close relationships with other people is always on their minds.[9]

> Loneliness is the first thing which God's eye named, not good.
>
> JOHN MILTON

We want to be wanted. We want to be connected. And deep in our hearts, we want to be known. Psychologists call it our "affiliative drive." And make no mistake: No one is too tough to go without belonging. The need to be known is not just an emotional desire to feel warm and accepted, however. It is literally a matter of life or death.

Two independent studies, one done at the University of California at Berkeley and the other at the University of Michigan, found that adults who do not cultivate nurturing relationships have death rates twice as high as those with frequent, caring contact.[10]

Nothing reaches so deeply into the human personality, tugs so tightly, as relationship. One reason for this is that it is only in the context of connection with others that our deepest needs are met.[11] We need camaraderie, affection, love. These are not merely options or sentimental trimmings in life; they are part of our survival kit. We *need* to be known.[12]

In chapter 3, we explored the value of owning our weakness. We focused on being honest with ourselves. In this chapter we focus on being honest with others, on being authentic. Why do we do that? Because there's power in being received for who we *really* are. There's strength to be had in being known.

LONELINESS SABOTAGES STRENGTH

In 1992, Michael Stipe and his band, R.E.M., recorded a song that touched a sensitive nerve. "Everybody Hurts" became an anthem for suffering souls of all ages who needed encouragement to "hang on."[13] The song ended with these words: *You are not alone.* Comfort and community are found in this simple sentence. But is it true? Not if you ask some people. Many of us, in pain, feel we are as isolated as Admiral Byrd on the ice barrier—even in our own hometowns.

> Live your life from your heart. Share from your heart. And your story will touch and heal people's souls.
>
> MELODY BEATTIE

Consider this: In 1985, when researchers asked a cross section of the American people, "How many confidants do you have?" the most common response to the question was three. Not too bad, right? But twenty years later, when researchers asked the same question, the most common response was none. One-quarter of us said we had no one at all with whom to talk openly and intimately.[14]

That's sad. Perhaps even sadder, however, is that even when

we *do* have friends and family to talk to, when we have spouses that share our lives, loneliness can still find its way into our relationships and make us feel distant and detached.

Does this matter? *Absolutely*. And here's the reason: Feelings of loneliness almost always sabotage our efforts to find a way through our hardships. Loneliness, for example, engenders depression. More than thirty million adults experience debilitating depression at some point in their lives.[15] And although some depression is the result of a chemical imbalance, much of our depression is the result of our reactions to life's hurtful circumstances.[16] And chief among those reactions is feeling lonely, as if nobody really understands or cares.[17]

Of course, *feeling* alone is not the same as *being* alone, or solitude. I want to make this clear. One drains our resources while the other multiplies them. When we *feel* alone, we feed our despair and self-doubt. When we *choose* to be alone, in solitude, for a time, we nourish our minds and spirits. When we *feel* alone, we are left empty and unfulfilled. When we *choose* to be alone, our solitude brings fulfillment and inspiration. So never confuse *feeling* alone with *being* alone. The two are at opposite ends of the emotional spectrum.

HOW FEELING CONNECTED MAKES US STRONGER

Experts agree that our social webs of connection fall into three categories: (1) *Intimate connectedness* that is up close and personal, (2) *relational connectedness* that has to do with a wider circle of friends and family, and (3) *collective connectedness* that comes from feeling a part of a large group, like an alumni association, a congregation, or a union. There is power in all three of these. And when even the thought of being disconnected from any one of them comes into play, we begin to lose our internal strength.

An innovative research team headed by Dr. Roy Baumeister,

of Florida State University, demonstrated this in a series of extensive studies on relationships. They began by rounding up undergraduate volunteers and asking them to complete two questionnaires. They then gave some of the students bogus results to bolster their level of confidence and comfort.[18] "You're lucky," some of the volunteers were told. "You're the type who'll have rewarding relationships throughout your life. Most likely, you'll have enduring friendships and a long and happy marriage, with plenty of people who'll always care deeply about you."

On another portion of the group, the researchers dropped a fairly large psychological bomb. "We hate to tell you this, but according to these results, you're the type who probably will end up alone. You may have friends and relationships now, but by your midtwenties, most of these will have drifted away. Relationships just won't last for you. Odds are, you'll end up more and more alone the longer you live."

> What makes loneliness an anguish is not that I have no one to share my burden, but this: I have only my own burden to bear.
>
> DAG HAMMARSKJOLD

For members of a third group, the research team provided feedback that was purposely off the point: "You're inherently accident prone," and so on. The reason for conveying this bad news was to create what psychologists call a "misfortune control condition." They wanted to sort out the effect of bad news in general from the effect of bad news pertaining to social connections.[19]

The participants were sorted into three categories: Future Alone, Future Belonging, and Misfortune Control. Then the real test began: Subjects were asked to describe their moods and then complete a list of questions requiring serious verbal and mathematical thinking.

When describing their moods, the Future Alone group, who had been given the bad news about their long-term social lives, indicated no emotional distress. But they performed significantly worse, in both speed and accuracy, on the questions than did the Future Belonging group, who got the rosy report about their relationships. The Future Alone group also scored worse than the Misfortune Control group (who had received dire predictions of physical calamities). Here's the point: Bad news alone does not diminish our cognitive capacities—but bad news about our social connections does. How does feeling disconnected from others affect us? In a series of follow-up studies, this same research team showed that even the *anticipation* of social disconnection leads to memory lapses, reduction in listening abilities, difficulty with impulse control, and an undermining of our ability to make helpful decisions.[20]

As you might have already anticipated, those who look forward to meaningful connections have stronger indicators on personal strength. They make wiser decisions, they persevere, they delay their gratification, and in one study, they even eat less-fattening foods.[21]

The bottom line of all this research is to underscore how personally empowering it is to live with a web of social connection—a community in which we are known. The mere thought of its fading causes diminished personal strength.

NOTHING WEAKENS US MORE THAN OUR SECRETS

Some time ago, I was speaking in Virginia and asked the audience of several hundred to close their eyes. I told them I wanted to pose a question and have them answer by raising their hands. As the audience closed their eyes, I asked, "How many of you are currently carrying something painful or walking through hardship that nobody knows about but you?"

Slowly, more than half of the audience quietly slipped their hands up and back down again. I was astonished. I had never asked an audience to do that before, and I hadn't known what to expect. I was literally dumbfounded for a moment. This was not a group that came together to talk about their pain. This was just a random gathering of churchgoers who came to hear a speaker on a Sunday morning.

> When we get too caught up in the busyness of the world, we lose connection with one another—and ourselves.
>
> JACK KORNFIELD

When I asked people to submit a card indicating what kind of pain they were carrying in private, they said things like the following:

- My wife had an affair.
- I have an eye disease.
- I'm drowning in debt.
- My husband verbally abuses me.
- My daughter is using drugs.
- My spouse and I are on the verge of separating.
- My house is about to be foreclosed.
- I contracted a sexually transmitted disease.
- My teenager won't talk to me.
- A friend betrayed me.

The numbers of cards with statements like these seemed endless.

Since that time, I've asked the same question of several more groups, and I now realize that the response is a predictable one. More than half the hands always go up. But I've also added a second question: "If you are carrying a private pain and also feeling lonely because of it, keep your hand up."

Almost the same number of hands remain raised. That's not surprising, I suppose. Psychiatrist Paul Tournier said, "Nothing makes us so lonely as our secrets." When we don't feel we can trust another person with the burden of our pain, we sentence ourselves to a kind of solitary confinement. Private pain and hidden hurts always make us weaker.

BEING KNOWN REQUIRES HONESTY

When an older man coaxed Jennifer, a first grader, away from her dolls one afternoon and fondled her, she kept the dirty secret to herself. She didn't tell anyone about the incident until she was twenty-one and engaged to be married. At that point, Jennifer felt she owed it to her fiancé to tell the story. What she didn't tell him, however, was that she still suffered flashbacks from the abuse. She could still feel the old man's repulsive touch, and she experienced a virtual cauldron of emotions: guilt, disgust, anger, shame. The feelings wouldn't let her go. And these same emotions were what kept her feeling isolated in the pain of this incident that had happened so long ago. Even though her husband knew what had happened, Jennifer didn't tell him about the emotions she still carried.

> Language has created the word "loneliness" to express the pain of being alone. And it has created the word "solitude" to express the glory of being alone.
>
> PAUL TILLICH

That's a common practice. For whatever reason, we sometimes hide our true feelings from those who are closest to us.[22] The feelings may be related to our sense of self-worth following a bad business decision or to our fears following a medical diagnosis made months ago. And when we conceal our feelings, we close the door to potential connections. We can't help but feel alone when we compartmentalize our feelings.

Wayne, a friend of mine, is a good example. As a child, he learned to bury his feelings. In his early teens he revealed his feelings about a struggle he was having, and he saw his coach roll his eyes at his colleague. I'm sure Wayne's coach thought he didn't see him, but Wayne did. And it shut him down immediately. Truth be told, it shut Wayne down for a long time. He didn't share his feelings ever again. He never talked about them, even to himself. Wayne anesthetized his feelings of pain through sports, sex, work, and sometimes even drugs. Not until he was feeling so low that he was considering harming himself, taking his own life, did Wayne show his emotions again.

Dreams and anguish bring us together.

EUGENE IONESCO

He discovered someone who had overcome the same kind of excruciating pain he was going through, and it was the first person he had met who he felt was willing to listen without judgment. He became instrumental in getting Wayne out of his paralyzing loneliness. How? By enabling Wayne to share his honest emotions.

Whenever we shut down our emotional warehouses and share only what we think others can handle or what seems appropriate, we conceal a primary pathway for others knowing and understanding our pain. In other words, when we quarantine our real emotions, we miss out on opportunities to stay connected.

THE TOXIC ASSET OF SUSPICION

Economists talk about toxic assets. These are assets that appear to have value but are actually liabilities. In the case of a bank, for example, toxic assets might be loans that appear to be valuable. But the homes that secured them have decreased below the value of the loan, making them toxic. In the end, toxic assets harm your bottom line.

The same is true in our personal lives. We sometimes hold on to toxic assets, believing they will benefit us, when in the end, they are actually harmful to us. A prime example is distrust. When we are hurting and feeling weak, distrust becomes a premium. After all, we don't want any more pain, so we are often tempted to hunker down and build up our defenses. One of the ways we do this is by keeping people at arm's length, guarding our hearts from potential harm, and maybe even shutting others out entirely. We fear what they might say or do to cause us further pain.

And, yes, sometimes these fears are warranted. If you have an insensitive relative who wants to preach you out of your pain or get you to "snap out of it" with tactless sayings, you have every right to set firm and healthy boundaries. What we are saying is this: Be careful when you build those boundaries so that you don't wall out others who can bring you genuine community. In other words, don't allow distrust to drive you into more isolation. George Eliot, in her novel *Middlemarch*, poses a good question: "What loneliness is more lonely than distrust?"

When Cindy became the victim of abuse in her marriage, she retreated from nearly everyone. Her friendships faded as her bruises became more defined. Her turmoil at home was private. Nobody knew. And the shame Cindy carried because of it was her abusive husband's insurance against being found out. Like countless other victims of abuse, Cindy decided to trust no one. She could have told her parents, her friends, her pastor, or a counselor. But she didn't. Her distrust of others who could have helped her outweighed the potential good of confiding. It kept her quiet. And that kept her frightfully alone.

I need to be honest here. Sometimes people are afraid to trust anyone with the truth about what they are suffering because when they have tried it in the past, their hearers responded with spiritual platitudes or a refusal to believe what the victims told them. That dismissal or suspicion of the one who has taken the risk of opening up pours salt in an already deep wound and does nothing more than ensure that victims will think twice before trusting anyone with the truth again.

But you don't have to experience abuse to start shutting down and distrusting people. Any number of things can cause us to put up emotional walls with other people. I know a man who had a series of interactions with coaches, camp counselors, and other adults, that eventually led him to wall off nearly all of his emotions.

He had grown up without a father and maybe, more important, without the blessing that can come from a father. So he craved the attention, the affirmation, of a male role model and a mentor. One day, as a teenager, he was trying to open up to two camp counselors as they were walking along a trail in the woods. He was walking slightly ahead of the two counselors and talking about what was going on inside of him. But as he looked over his shoulder, one of the counselors, who did not notice that he was looking back, made a dismissive gesture to the other. That was all the convincing this teenager needed to keep his feelings inside and not open up to anyone. Do you know the feeling? Have you been keeping your true feelings buried?

> We cannot live only for ourselves. A thousand fibers connect us with our fellow men.
>
> HERMAN MELVILLE

You may think that being suspicious of others in your time of personal suffering is a way of protecting yourself against further hardship, but it is almost sure to be a toxic asset. It's far better to seek those who are trustworthy and trust them as much as your heart is able.

BEING REAL IS MORE IMPORTANT THAN BEING RIGHT

"The surest cure for vanity is loneliness," said American novelist Thomas Wolfe. It's tough to maintain your pride when you are feeling all alone. Yet sometimes, in our despair, we actually become prideful about our suffering. We have a tough time accepting others. We play what some have called the "pain game," comparing our own suffering with that of others and making light of their trials by comparing them with our own. Of course, comparison doesn't give us comfort. Quite the opposite. It actually drives us further apart.

You are far more apt to find community when you accept the fact that although we have countless differences, we all have one thing in common: We all know what it means to hurt. Tears are the same for all of us. Once we accept this, we accept others with more grace, and we lean into a deeper connection. In other words, we find community in acceptance.

Rachel, the victim of identity theft, experienced month upon month of intense anxiety. Everything from her credit to her insurance was in question, and there was little she could do about it. She spent countless hours doing everything within her power to curtail the effects of the theft, and the stress from the crisis eventually led to a full-blown panic disorder.

At the same time, Nancy, a work colleague and friend of Rachel, was going through her own crisis, which started just a bit before Rachel's. Nancy had been diagnosed with Stage III breast cancer. "I've got to be honest," she confided. "When I first learned of Rachel's troubles, I didn't have much sympathy." She went on to describe how her pain of possible death dwarfed Rachel's pain of financial troubles and panic attacks. ("I'd trade my problem in for hers in a second.") But something shifted in Nancy's spirit one night when she witnessed one of Rachel's panic attacks as they were walking to their cars in the parking lot after work. As Nancy attempted to comfort Rachel, she realized just how devastating this panic disorder was to Rachel. She saw the same kind of fear and agony in Rachel that she had in herself. And in that moment, Nancy realized she had no right to discount Rachel's pain and suffering. "I was close to writing off my good friend before that happened," Nancy continued. "I was shutting her out because her pain didn't measure up to mine. Of course, I now see that's ridiculous. Pain is pain. Her pain is as legitimate as mine. And accepting that fact gave me my friend back."

Sure, you may have a right to single out your pain and suffering as being more unbearable than anyone else's, but in doing so, you only distance yourself from the people you need the most. "If you are afraid of being lonely," said French author Jules Renard, "don't try to be right."

There's a difference between being genuine with your feelings (which is imperative to progress) and being haughty with them. It comes down to the difference between a prideful spirit and a humble spirit. Both can be honest. But trivializing other people's suffering because yours is far worse gets you no closer to moving past the pain of isolation to eventual healing. Humility, and not the false kind, is the only antidote to the smugness of intolerable suffering and the only path to genuine acceptance of others. And it's that acceptance that ultimately provides you with community.

JELLYFISH IN ARMOR

"You're the first person I have ever been completely honest with." Every psychologist hears these words from time to time, but it was Sidney Jourard who made sense of them in his in-depth book *The Transparent Self*. Puzzling, isn't it? Clients and patients will be more honest and authentic with a therapist or a clinician than they are with family or friends. Jourard concluded that each of us has a built-in desire to be known, but we often stifle our vulnerability out of fear. We're afraid of rejection.

> Silence is a danger to the weak. For the things I was prompted to keep silent about were nearly always the things I was ashamed of, which would have been far better aired.
>
> JOANNA FIELD

The result? We wear masks. We put up our guard. We become what Abraham Maslow called "jellyfish in armor." Consider the words of this letter. The author is unknown, but the letter could easily have been written by any of us:

> Don't be fooled by me. Don't be fooled by the face I wear. I wear a mask. I wear a thousand masks—masks that I am afraid to take off; and none of them are me.
>
> Pretending is an art that is second nature to me, but don't be fooled. For my sake, don't be fooled. I give the impression that I am secure, that all is sunny and unruffled within me as well as without; that confidence is my name and coolness my game; that the water is calm and I am in command; and that I need no one. But don't believe me, please. My surface may seem smooth, but my surface is my mask, my ever varying and ever concealing mask.

The writer goes on to confess that underneath the mask is no smugness, no complacence, only confusion, fear, aloneness, and sheer panic at the thought of being exposed. Then this piercing paragraph:

> Who am I, you may wonder. I am someone you know very well. For I am every man you meet. I am every woman you meet. I am right in front of you.[23]

Why do all of us hide behind masks? We vacillate between the impulse to reveal ourselves and the impulse to protect ourselves. Why?

The primary reason we wear our masks, however, is to guard against rejection. *If people knew the real me, they'd never accept me,* we say to ourselves. So we slip behind a self-made facade and pretend. Sociologists call it impression management; the rest of us call it pain.

If we wear our masks long enough, we may guard against rejection, and we may even be admired, but we'll never be whole. We'll never be strong. And that means we'll never enjoy true intimacy.

In *Traveling Mercies*, Anne Lamott writes, "Everything is usually so masked or perfumed or disguised in the world, and it's so touching when you get to see something real and human . . . no matter how neurotic the member [of the group], how deeply annoying or dull . . . when people have seen you at your worst, you don't have to put on the mask as much. And that gives us license to try on that radical hat of liberation, that hat of self-acceptance."[24]

> If we wear a mask that says, "I'm tough," we don't have to worry about admitting how weak and frightened we really are.
>
> CHARLES SWINDOLL

ADMITTING YOU HAVE A DARK SIDE

That "radical hat of liberation," as Lamott calls it, is felt most deeply when we admit our worst weaknesses. Talking freely about our failures is therapeutic. After all, the strongest people, the healthiest and happiest, are not exempt from miserable parts. When we confess our dark sides to others, we find healing.[25]

I'll be honest. I'll put it in print and publish it in a book. I confess that I have tendencies toward meanness, selfishness, envy, materialism, cruelty, dishonesty, lust, and all the rest. And so does everyone else. We all have some degree of these miserable parts. But here's what's important: The more we bring them into the open, the stronger our potential for goodness is.

How can this be? Because our character is not hammered out in the *absence* of negative traits but *because* of them. Our struggle to overcome selfishness, for example, will make our generous spirit, once honed, far more prized, meaningful, and valuable than if it had come more easily or more naturally. There is no virtue in not acting on a desire that doesn't exist.

> There is a sacredness in tears. They are not the mark of weakness, but of power.
>
> WASHINGTON IRVING

Yet so many people, especially those who are well-intentioned, work diligently to block or bury their baser parts from being known by other people. They operate under the false assumption that if they ignore such bad tendencies, their dark sides will disappear. Of course, that doesn't work. Stronger people come to terms with their rotten parts, eventually learning why they have them and, most important, how to transform them as best they can.

It all begins with an honest confession: "I've got to tell you, I really struggle with celebrating somebody else's success," we might say. That's all. That is enough to test the waters and see whether we can risk going further.

The point is that we will never be known until we share the parts of our hearts that hurt or the parts of our hearts that hide— the dark parts. Either way, sharing those parts is a risk. But facing this danger is a prerequisite to being known. And it's a requirement for being loved.

THE ONLY PATH TOWARD LOVE

Do you remember the classic children's book *The Velveteen Rabbit*, by Margery Williams? Perhaps this line from the old toy horse will refresh your memory:

> "Real isn't how you are made. It's a thing that happens to you," said the toy horse. "When a child loves you for a long, long time, not just to play with, but really loves you, then you become Real."

We are most real when we are most known and loved. And here's the secret: The more real we become, the more love we experience. And the more love we experience, the more real we become.

The toy rabbit didn't know real rabbits even existed. He thought they were all stuffed with sawdust like he was. "And he understood that sawdust was quite out-of-date and should never be mentioned in modern circles." The rabbit kept authenticity at bay through his fear of being found out. He never wanted to risk being *really* known. And yet authenticity is the only way to be loved.

That's the irony. We fear that being known will lead to rejection. It will get our vulnerable hearts kicked across the floor. But it is only by being known that our hearts are truly loved.

> Mutual empathy is the great unsung human gift.
>
> JEAN BAKER MILLER

C. S. Lewis, as he so often does, puts his finger on a truth that resonates:

> To love at all is to be vulnerable. Love anything, and your heart will certainly be wrung and possibly broken. If you want to make sure of keeping it intact, you must give your heart to no one, not even an animal. Wrap it carefully round with hobbies and little luxuries, avoid all entanglements; lock it up safe in the casket or coffin of your selfishness. But in that casket—safe, dark, motionless, airless—it will change. It will not be broken; it will become unbreakable, impenetrable, irredeemable. . . . The only place outside of heaven where you can be perfectly safe from all the dangers and perturbations of love is Hell.[26]

Nobody wants a hard-boiled heart. And yet each time we pass up an opportunity to be known, we face a greater danger than having our hearts rejected. We risk a hardened heart that even guards against the risk of love.

THE SACRED SPACE BETWEEN US

"Who weeps for you?" I have a friend who is fond of asking that question. It's his way of helping people identify who really loves them. And I've seen grown men break down as they try to answer. It's a piercing question because it immediately reveals just how lonely we can be when we aren't willing to risk the possibility of being shut down or rejected.

Research on crying has shown that tears contain chemicals related to stress and depression. When people cry, they are actually washing away harmful effects of hormones. They are becoming stronger.[27] Regardless of the biological benefits related to shedding a few tears, crying with someone who cares is one of the greatest bonding agents we humans possess. It not only cleanses the body but also connects our hearts. Kahlil Gibran says, "You never forget the ones with whom you have wept."

He could have also said you never forget the ones *for* whom you have wept. Of course, this is not to be taken too literally. Sharing tears is not the ultimate sign of connection. The true indicator of a deep and powerful bond is found when spiritual encouragement fills the space between us. Ralph Waldo Emerson put it this way: "The glory of friendship is not the outstretched hand, nor the kindly smile, nor the joy of companionship; it is the spiritual inspiration that comes to one when he discovers that someone else believes in him and is willing to trust him."

When you get inside the life of another person, and you allow that person to get inside yours, and you feel each other's hurts, and you know each other's hearts, you are on track with the ultimate meaning and power of the universe.

When Martin Buber, the great Jewish philosopher and

theologian, was asked, "Where is God?" he was wise enough not to give the cliché answer: God is everywhere. Buber, instead, would answer that God is found in relationships. God fills the space between us. God infuses our connections with power. And that is why there's strength in being known.

FOR REFLECTION

1. When are you most likely to feel lonely? What are the predictable circumstances, and what could you do to minimize them?

2. Do you agree that keeping personal secrets (about ourselves) makes us weaker? What secrets do you think you could appropriately divulge, and how do you think it might lighten your heart and make you stronger to do so?

3. How willing are you to honestly explore your dark side with other people? What's your greatest fear in exposing it? And what is the potential gain for you in doing so?

4. How does the concept of "sacredness in the spaces between us" strike you? Do you ever sense a holiness as a result of your connections with others? If not, why not? If so, how would you describe it?

WORKBOOK EXERCISE 4

If you are using the optional workbook, the exercise for this chapter will show you how to build stronger connections with others. It will help you inventory the places in your life that keep you from building bridges, and it will give you tools for being truly known by those who love and support you.

MAKING IT REAL
LEVERAGING THE POWER OF YOUR HEART

Go to your bosom; Knock there, and ask your heart what it doth know.

—WILLIAM SHAKESPEARE, *MEASURE FOR MEASURE*

If you were to take Shakespeare's advice, what would your heart have to say? For that matter, now that you've read the previous two chapters, what does your heart know? Does it know how to leverage the strength of feeling vulnerable or the strength of feeling connected? I hope so. But I hope for more than that. I hope that you will take what you now know and apply it to your life.

Your heart may feel broken by a dream that has been dashed against the hard realities of some pain or difficulty you never expected to face. If so, the power you can find in your broken heart can see you through it. And if your heart has slowly grown weak because of a dream you've shelved too long, you can restore its strength and experience its vibrancy once more.

"Inaction breeds doubt and fear," said Dale Carnegie. "Action breeds confidence and courage." In the search for strength you didn't know you have, success comes from putting what you've just read into action.

ARE YOU USING THE POWER OF YOUR HEART?

Just as I did in the conclusion of part 1, I want to again offer you a brief assessment that will help to improve your self-awareness in this area too. So before I highlight some practical applications of the material, you may want to complete this simple questionnaire of just ten items.

Take your time, and be honest as you consider your responses. There are no right or wrong answers. Just answer yes, no, or maybe to each.

1. I feel it's often best to ignore my weak spots.
   Yes ____ No ____ Maybe ____

2. I feel deeply known by at least three people outside my family.
   Yes ____ No ____ Maybe ____

3. It's difficult for me to admit that I need help.
   Yes ____ No ____ Maybe ____

4. I have a dark, personal secret that I keep to myself.
   Yes ____ No ____ Maybe ____

5. I seldom invite feedback from others about my flaws.
   Yes ____ No ____ Maybe ____

6. I tend to share only those things about myself that I think people want to hear.
   Yes ____ No ____ Maybe ____

7. I'm content to remain unaware of my shortcomings.
   Yes ___ No ___ Maybe ___

8. I tend to be suspicious of others and find it hard to trust them.
   Yes ___ No ___ Maybe ___

9. My unhealthy pride often keeps me from seeing myself accurately.
   Yes ___ No ___ Maybe ___

10. I often wear a mask because I would rather be liked than be known.
    Yes ___ No ___ Maybe ___

MAKING SENSE OF YOUR RESULTS

Give yourself 2 for every yes, 0 for every no, and 1 for every maybe. Your score will fall somewhere between 0 and 20 points.

If you scored *between 15 and 20*, you can significantly improve the power of your heart. While you may be feeling quite powerless now, you will see dramatic advances in your sense of well-being when you apply the principles you've learned in this section of the book. There's no need to feel overwhelmed. Taking a few small action steps, noted on the following pages, will set you on the right path to leveraging the power of your heart—even if you are not optimistic.

If you scored *between 6 and 14*, you are likely to vacillate between leveraging the power of your heart and overlooking it. That is, sometimes you find great strength because you are leaning into your capacity to feel vulnerable and to own your weakness, while at other times you're likely to hide from or dismiss feelings of weakness. In the same way, you are sometimes more inclined to keep your true self hidden from others. You'll want to pay special attention to the practical helps that follow in order to more consistently harness the power that comes from feeling vulnerable and feeling connected.

If you scored *between 0 and 5*, your heart is in prime condition to leverage the power that comes from feeling vulnerable and feeling connected. Take advantage of the practical applications that follow to hone your heart's strength. In fact, you'll find a suggestion, specifically for you, for doing just that.

GETTING PERSONAL

Now that you have this bit of self-awareness in hand, I want to help you take what you have read in part 2 and apply it to the areas in your life where you will gain the most benefit. Because I know that every reader is coming to this book with unique challenges, I again encourage you to view the following suggestions as items on a menu. Select those that appeal to you, and focus on putting them into practice.

LEVERAGING THE POWER OF FEELING VULNERABLE

In chapter 3 you saw how feeling vulnerable helps you to find personal strength—how owning your weakness makes you stronger. Here are a few practical ways of making this real in your own life:

◆ Identify Your Achilles' Heel

The large tendon connecting muscles in the lower leg with the heel bone is known as the Achilles tendon, after the character in Homer's Greek drama *The Iliad*. Achilles's mother held her infant son by the heel and dipped him in the river Styx. Achilles's heel became his one vulnerable spot. Sometimes we refer to an area of vulnerability as a person's "fatal weakness," or "fatal flaw." We all have one, whether we admit it or not. Of course, admitting it can be a challenge for some people. Other people know it immediately. If you fall into the former group, I recommend that you give serious thought to the one thing you'd most like to change about your personal character qualities. Maybe you would like to be more patient, more generous, more forgiving, and so on. In other words, identify the chink in the armor of your personality. What's your weak point? Are you willing to admit it? How about your top three? I'm not going to challenge you here to improve them. I simply want you to *own* them. You can do this by writing a paragraph or so about each one. Journal your thoughts on why you think these are sources of weakness for you. Describe how each one of them is typically exhibited in your life. Simply writing a paragraph or so about each weakness will cause you to own it more fully.

◆ Let Your Heart Be True

What is your predominant emotion right now? Can you put your finger on that feeling with ease? Most of us have to think about that. Emotional awareness doesn't always come easy. What *does* come easy is denial. We humans frequently bury emotions that make us feel ashamed or uncomfortable. We sometimes trade what we *are* feeling for what we think we *should* be feeling, and that always leads to a lack of internal clarity and awareness. So here's something you might consider: In the big picture of your emotional world, what is the one emotion you are most likely to deny—and why? Is it anger, inadequacy, envy, sadness, disappointment? What feeling do you tend to repress whenever it tries to appear? Think about why that is. Perhaps you received a message as a child about that particular emotion. Maybe you've been burned in a relationship because of that feeling. Only you know—even if you may try to ignore it—but why don't you make today the day you own that feeling? You can do so not only by identifying it but also by intentionally putting yourself in a place where you know that feeling is likely to bubble up. Is that too scary? If so, for now, just identify the emotion and be intentional about giving yourself permission to feel it the next time it arises.

◆ Smoke Out Your Deepest Weakness

In chapter 3, we identified unhealthy pride as a bloated ego, laced with arrogance and conceit. We called it the deepest weakness in every heart, not because all of us are egomaniacs, but because almost all of us have a tendency to look down on other people for one reason or another. We don't like to admit that, but it's true. So let's get personal. Knowing that all of us have pride in our hearts, when is your unhealthy pride most likely to make itself known? In other words, what circumstances bring your feelings of arrogance to the surface: Does it happen when another person is incompetent? When someone doesn't understand a current event the same way you do? When someone isn't as spiritually in tune as you believe you are? When someone doesn't share your political or social cause? Your heart knows, so can you admit it to yourself? Can you examine it without trying to pretend that it doesn't exist? Remember, if you think you don't have "too much of that" in your own heart, you are in denial. Don't allow that to be the case. Confess your pride in specific terms—the when, the why, and the how of it—if only to yourself.

◆ Seek Wise Counsel

Benjamin Franklin said, "He that won't be counseled can't be helped." He had a point. If you want to take a daring step toward feeling vulnerable, what would you think of the idea of seeing a competent counselor to help you unearth your insecurities? Some people view the idea of getting professional help as a weakness. Okay. What if it is? The whole point of owning your weakness is to find strength. For many people, one of the best ways to do that is to consult a professional—someone who is trained and adept at helping you peel away the layers of pride and denial to expose what's really going on inside you—your fears, your inadequacies, your anxieties. Does that sound scary? It may be. But if you are serious about leveraging the power of your heart, you are likely to need a guide to help you tend to both your wounds and your fears. Seeing a counselor is one of the bravest steps you may ever take on your journey to feel vulnerable. By the way, speaking with a counselor need not be a long-term commitment. You may elect to see someone for just a few weeks. That's up to you. The goal is to have that person help you set aside your unhealthy pride so that you can fully own your weakness.

LEVERAGING THE POWER OF FEELING CONNECTED

In chapter 4, you saw how personal strength is found whenever you feel connected—how you can find strength in being known. Here are a few practical ways of doing that:

◆ Start a Small Group

Being in a small group is one of the best ways to feel connected. This is a group of at least three other people who meet once a week, every other week, or once a month for the purpose of being known to one another. The members of the group may read a book and discuss it. They may choose to use a study guide with questions. They may meet with no other agenda but to be connected. If you are not already part of a small group, I urge you to consider starting one. This may sound intimidating, but it's actually quite easy. Begin by thinking of a half dozen people or so who you think would make up a good group. They don't even have to know one another. Let these people know what you have in mind, and see whether they are interested in being part of a group. Schedule your first meeting together, and discuss what they might like the group to look like. That's it. If you feel shy about initiating it yourself, ask one of your friends to join you in making it happen. The little amount of effort you will exert to get this going will likely pay you back with big dividends. A small group of people on whom you can lean for support is a foundation for leveraging your heart and feeling connected.

◆ Shed Light on Your Dark Side

Does anyone you know like to expose his or her ugly side? Think of a scenario in which one person "loses it" with another and then realizes everyone else is watching. *Ouch!* But everyone has a part that isn't pretty—including you. It's the part of you that you don't like—and you certainly don't want others to see it if you can help it. In fact, you probably keep it stuffed down inside as much as possible. Maybe it's your impatience, your quick temper, your stinginess, your materialism, or your irresponsibility. If you'd like to gain some control over it and weaken its power, however, try this: Confess it to someone. You can do this in nearly any relationship—with your friends one-on-one or in a group. You can even tell strangers about your dark side. Try it. The result is almost guaranteed: They will reveal a bit of their dark sides too. Why would they do that? Because vulnerability begets vulnerability. Once you share something about yourself that you're not proud of, you become approachable and safe to others. Not only that, but that piece of you that you don't like often becomes smaller in the act of sharing it. So here's my suggestion: Note a couple of aspects you don't like about yourself, and share them with someone, a stranger or a friend, in the next forty-eight hours.

◆ Take Off Your Mask

Everyone wears "masks" on occasion. We wear them to guard against feeling judged or viewed negatively. But once we feel safe enough to remove our masks and be known for who we really are, we find more strength. Our relationships become more authentic and healthier. So here's my suggestion: Label a couple of masks you sometimes wear in front of other people, and identify those circumstances in which you are most apt to wear them. For example, maybe you wear a "cool" mask when you are actually feeling quite nervous. And maybe you wear it most often when you are about to give a presentation at work. What would happen if you were to take off that mask? What if you were to admit to the group that you were feeling a bit uneasy about making the presentation because you fear being seen in a certain way? Could it be that this kind of vulnerability would actually endear you to your coworkers? I'm not telling you to automatically do this, just to think it through. Why? Because sometimes our different roles as employees or parents, or what have you, require us to put on certain faces. In contrast, the interpersonal *masks* I'm talking about are those that keep you from being truly known—especially by people you care about. So, again, identify a few masks that you wear frequently, and consider what might happen if you were to remove them at the appropriate places.

◆ Share a Secret

You've heard the statement before: "We're only as sick as our secrets." Well, then, what are yours? What are you hoping people never find out about you? That's a scary question, we know. It's as personal as it gets. After all, we keep personal secrets out of shame, embarrassment, or fear of rejection. But keeping secrets leads to increased stress and anxiety. Secrets deplete our strength. So again I ask, what are some of yours? Maybe you were abused in your past. Maybe you struggle with an addiction or a compulsive behavior that no one knows about. Maybe you routinely cheat others. Maybe it's the burden of guilt over a private indiscretion from your past. Maybe it is an ugly, secret wish that harm will come to someone you dislike. Maybe it's a misperception others have about you that you've never corrected. Perhaps it's just plain old insecurity that nobody knows about. Whatever it is, you will discover a surprising relief of tension in your heart when you unload a secret you've been hiding. In fact, research shows that the simple task of writing down a secret, even if no one ever reads it, makes people feel better. Are you willing to take that step? Can you make a list of three or four secrets that only you know about? Are you willing to take the courageous step of unloading one of them with a trusted confidant?

PART 3
THE POWER OF YOUR SOUL

You don't have *a soul. . . . You* are *a soul.*
You have *a body.*
—WALTER M. MILLER JR.

I've talked about the power of your mind in part 1 and the power of your heart in part 2. Both of these, the brain (or mind) and the heart, are relatively easy to locate and describe. But the soul? That's a different story.

The 2003 film *21 Grams*, starring Sean Penn and Naomi Watts, got its title from research done in 1907 that attempted to prove the existence of the human soul by recording the loss of a small amount of body weight (twenty-one grams) at the moment of death. The researcher's conclusions were discounted by the scientific community, even at the time, but the idea took root in the culture of the day. Twenty-one grams is the approximate weight of five nickels or a hummingbird or, if you had believed the conclusion of the 1907 research, the weight of the human soul.[1] Of course, there was no way to prove the doctor's findings. He didn't use the scientific method in his research, and it's not possible to take an X-ray of the soul. You can't examine it under a microscope.

But that hasn't kept some people from trying to sell their souls—literally. An eighteen-year-old once put his soul up for auction on eBay. Within a few days, eBay removed his offer and alerted him that eBay did not allow the auctioning of human souls.[2] *Wired* magazine reported that a twenty-nine-year-old university communications instructor was successful in his attempt to sell his immortal soul. After a ten-day bidding war, a New York real-estate agent purchased it for $1,325.[3]

If that doesn't leave you scratching your head, maybe a few abstractions on the human soul from some of the world's great thinkers will. Plato called it the "essence" of a person. Philosopher and theologian Thomas Aquinas viewed the soul as immortal. Augustine saw the soul as "a special substance, endowed with reason, adapted to rule the body."[4]

An immortal essence made of a special substance? That's getting pretty ethereal. Even the pragmatic thinker C. S. Lewis seemed a tad airy when he said, "Your soul has a curious shape because it is a hollow made to fit a particular swelling in the infinite contours of the Divine substance."[5] As I said, the soul is hazy. But maybe that's the point. Perhaps it is in our intangible spirits, our unearthly souls, where we come closest to finding a strength and a power we can barely articulate. A. W. Tozer said that apart from God himself, the human soul was the nearest thing to God. No wonder we struggle to describe it.

Whether we can clearly explain its form and articulate its existence or not, almost everyone believes in the existence of the soul. Even among non-churchgoing people, according to one national poll, more than three-fourths believe the soul lives on after death.[6] Philosophers and theologians can debate its mystical nuances, but for mere mortals, the human soul is something imperative to who we are. When J. R. R. Tolkien was being interviewed in 1955 for a *New York Times Book Review*, he was asked what made him tick. The then relatively obscure author responded: "I don't tick. I'm not a machine."[7] None of us wants to be viewed as a measly machine. Our very *being*, our "essence," is much deeper than mere mechanics. As Lewis said, we *are* souls.

Whatever your particular view of the soul, nearly everyone agrees that souls have been with us from the very beginning—as long as humans have walked the planet: "GOD formed Man out of dirt from the ground and blew into his nostrils the breath of life. The Man came alive—a living soul!"[8]

After nine seasons, the popular sitcom *Everybody Loves Raymond* broadcast its final episode. The star of the show, Ray Romano, had gone from being a struggling stand-up comedian to one of the highest-paid actors on television. At the conclusion of the last day's filming, Romano spoke to the studio audience, reflecting on his past and his future. He read from a note his brother had stuck in his luggage the day he moved from New York to Hollywood, nine years earlier.

"My older brother Richard wrote, 'What does it profit a man, if he gains the whole world, and loses his soul?'" said a tearful Romano. "Now I'm going to work on my soul."

In a sense, this final section of the book will help you do the same.

BE EMPTIED AND BE BOLD

Chapters 5 and 6 will show you how to find the power residing in your soul. They will uncover the strength you have in the spirit of your being.

Chapter 5, "Be Emptied," promotes the most radical and revolutionary way of finding strength: surrender. After all, who equates that with power? Surrendering is most commonly thought of as giving up. The universal symbol is a white flag hoisted above the head and waved in a downcast spirit of defeat. So if you're suspicious of this notion that there's strength in surrender, I understand. I just ask that you journey with me as I explore the idea that an unclenched fist just might hold the secret to the most amazing power you've ever experienced. In this chapter I will show you how being emptied of yourself releases a burden in your soul and infuses your spirit with a power you may never have known before.

Chapter 6, "Be Bold," is a call to action. At one point in the movie version of the Lord of the Rings trilogy, Sam is trying to encourage Frodo not to give up. He reminds Frodo that all the great stories are about characters who keep going when it seems too hard. They all find something to hang on to. "And what about us?" Frodo asks. "What do we have to hang on to?" Sam responds, "That there's good in the world. And it's worth fighting for." Chapter 6 is a call to fight for the goodness in your life. It's a call to be a little less sensible and a bit more risky. Why? Because an overcautious spirit drains us of passion. It happens gradually, mind you. Just a little bit of your spirit dies each day that goes by without an uplift of passion. But once you find a passion born of deep commitment, your soul is set on fire. You become bolder than you ever knew you were. And that gives you strength you didn't know you had.

IT IS WELL WITH MY SOUL

In the autumn of 1873, Horatio Spafford, a wealthy Chicago lawyer, placed his wife, Anna, and their four children on the *Ville du Havre* sailing from New York to France. He was forced to stay in the United States for several more weeks to settle some business matters before he could join the family in Europe.

The evening of November 21 found the *Ville du Havre* prow-east toward France on a calm Atlantic. The journey was progressing beautifully. A few hours later, about two o'clock in the morning on November 22, the *Ville du Havre* was carrying its sleeping passengers over a quiet sea when two terrific claps like thunder were followed by frightening screams. The engine stopped, the ship stood still. Passageways were filled with terrified, half-dressed people shouting questions that no one could answer. The *Ville du Havre* had been rammed by the English vessel, the *Lochearn*.

Mrs. Spafford saw three of her children swept away by the sea while she stood clutching the youngest child. Suddenly, she felt her baby torn violently from her arms. She reached out through the water and caught little Tanetta's gown. For a minute she held her again. Then the cloth wrenched from her hand. She reached out again and touched a man's leg in corduroy trousers. She became unconscious. She awoke later, finding that she had been rescued by sailors from the *Lochearn*. But her four children were gone.

In the meantime, Horatio Spafford was back in the United States, desperate to receive news of his family. Finally, a cable arrived from Wales stating that the four daughters were lost at sea, but his wife was still alive. He was crushed with what had happened. All night he walked the floor in anguish.

On the way across the Atlantic to join his wife, the captain announced that they were now passing the place where the *Ville du Havre* was wrecked. For Horatio Spafford, this was passing through the valley of the shadow of death. He sat down in his cabin on the high seas, near the place where his children perished, and wrote the words that are sung by so many who find comfort in the great hymn, "It Is Well with My Soul."[9]

How can this be? How can a man who has suffered such unspeakable loss find strength deep down in his soul? I dedicate the next two chapters to finding out.

5

BE EMPTIED
THERE'S STRENGTH IN SURRENDER

*The greatness of a man's power
is the measure of his surrender.*
—WILLIAM BOOTH

Maybe you've heard of the following strategy. It's clever. And it always works. In parts of India and Africa that are overrun with monkeys, officials control the monkey population by employing the help of professional monkey catchers who actually allow the monkeys to catch themselves.

Here's how they do it: A catcher hollows out a gourd no bigger than a basketball and cuts an opening into the gourd, about the size of a silver dollar. He carries the gourd to an area frequented by monkeys. Before placing the gourd on the ground in an open area near a tree, he holds the gourd above his head for all the monkeys to see. He then tethers the gourd, tying it so that its movement is restricted and it can't be carried off.

In plain view of all the monkeys, the monkey catcher then walks over to a banana tree and selects a banana. He holds it high above his head for the monkeys to see. Then he places it in the gourd and retreats several paces, out of sight from the monkeys.

What happens next is startling. A curious monkey will come over to the gourd, examine it, give it a push, and check out the banana within. There are bananas all around, all easily obtainable. But the monkey wants *that* banana. He can easily put his hand into the small opening of the gourd, and he can easily take it back out—as long as he's not grasping the banana. But as long as the monkey holds on to the banana, his tight fist around the banana is trapped in the gourd.

You might think the monkey would simply let go so he could be free, but he doesn't. He holds on to what he wants. He makes noises, jumps around, and shakes the gourd, but he won't release his grip on the banana, and that makes it easy to catch him. The monkey could have all the bananas he can eat hanging on trees, but he gets it into his head that he's got to have that solitary banana in the gourd. And he won't let go—literally.

That phenomenon isn't limited to monkeys, by the way. German theologian Helmut Thielicke described the experience of a child who had shoved his hand into the opening of an expensive Chinese vase and couldn't pull it out again. Parents and neighbors tugged on the child's arm, with the poor child continuing to howl. Finally, there was nothing left to do but to break the beautiful vase. "And then as the mournful heap of shards lay there," said Thielicke, "it became clear why the child had been so hopelessly stuck. His little fist grasped a paltry penny which he had spied in the bottom of the vase and which he, in his childish ignorance, would not let go."[1]

This chapter is dedicated to emptying that clenched fist of the

> If you surrender completely to the moments as they pass, you live more richly those moments.
>
> ANN MORROW LINDBERGH

childish impulse within us all. Why? Because there is strength in letting go. As you're about to see, there is radical power in surrender.

LOSING YOUR LIFE TO FIND IT?

Bernard Rimland earned his PhD at Pennsylvania State University and was on a fast track as a research psychologist. But three years later, in 1956, he hit a bump in the road. His son, Mark, was born and diagnosed with what was then a little-known disorder called autism. In fact, at the time, Dr. Rimland, like most, had never heard the term.

Thus began Dr. Rimland's quest to understand autism. He devoted much of his career to it, writing one of the first books on the topic and, in 1967, establishing the Autism Research Institute. Along the way, Rimland did a simple experiment that sheds some light on one of the great paradoxical truths of the ages: To find your life, you must lose it.

He asked 216 students to list the initials of ten people they knew best, which yielded a grand list of some two thousand people. He then asked them to indicate whether each person on their lists seemed happy or not. Finally, he asked them to go over their lists again and this time to indicate whether each person seemed selfish or unselfish. In other words, was the person interested mostly in his or her own desires or was he or she willing to be inconvenienced by others and their desires?

The striking result was that 70 percent of those judged unselfish seemed happy, while 95 percent of those judged selfish seemed *un*happy. Dr. Rimland was surprised by the paradox: "Selfish people are, by definition, those whose activities are devoted to *bringing themselves happiness*. Yet, at least as judged by others, these selfish people are far less likely to be happy than those whose efforts are devoted to making others happy."[2]

This finding begins to get at what "being emptied" does in

a person's life. It sheds light on the idea of discovering meaning beyond the self by being emptied. Emptied of what? Of the burden we so often carry—*the burden of needing to get our own way.*

It's the burden and tension of holding on to our lives with clenched fists.

> **Our anxiety does not empty tomorrow of its sorrow, but only empties today of its strength.**
>
> CHARLES H. SPURGEON

Let's face it: We are often obsessed with the desire that our lives go the way we want them to go. To give up that desire, to surrender it, is to give away our lives.[3] We can spend weeks, sometimes years, in a perpetual stew because something did not go as we wished. We fuss and fume. But when we empty ourselves of this compulsive need to have our own way—when we lose our lives, as it were—something almost mystical takes place deep within our souls—we find our real lives. When we hold our desires loosely, a massive burden is released, and a new happiness is found. It's what philosopher and Roman emperor Marcus Aurelius was getting at when he said, "To live happily is an inward power of the soul." When we surrender our selfishness, we are no longer limited to defining our happiness by merely getting what we want. Emptying ourselves of the burden to always get our way frees our souls.

FREE AT LAST

When you help other people, when you make someone else's way a little easier, you immediately receive a payoff yourself. George Burton Adams, an American educator and historian, said it nicely: "Note how good you feel after you have encouraged someone else. No other argument is necessary to suggest that you should never miss the opportunity to give encouragement." Ralph Waldo Emerson put it this way: "You cannot sincerely help another without helping yourself." And he could not have been more right. When we empty ourselves of our self-centered desires, when we surrender our desires to get our way, we are filled with grace. Each act of kindness, each act of self-giving love, expands our lives.

Numerous studies find that the ability to practice appreciation and love is the *defining* mark of the happiest human beings. When people engage in self-giving love by doing something extraordinarily positive, they use higher-level brain functions and set off a series of neurochemical reactions that shower their systems in positive emotions.

Perhaps you are wondering if this kind of happiness is triggered just as readily by having fun as it is by an act of self-giving love.[4] Martin Seligman, of the University of Pennsylvania, wondered the same thing. He gave his students an assignment that I've replicated in my own university classes. He asked them to engage in one pleasurable activity and one self-giving activity. Simple enough. But then he had them write about both. That's when they discovered that the pleasurable activity of hanging out with friends, watching a movie, or eating chocolate paled in comparison with the effects of the loving action. Seligman states that "when our philanthropic acts were spontaneous . . . the whole day went better." He goes on to say that self-giving love "consists in total engagement and in the loss of self-consciousness."[5] Time stops when we lend a helping hand, nurture a hurting soul, or offer a listening ear.

IT NEVER FAILS

When we empty ourselves, we make room in our souls for love—the ultimate power. It lifts us outside ourselves. It helps us see beyond the normal range of human vision—and over walls of resentment and barriers of betrayal. Love rises above the petty demands and conflicts of life and inspires our spirits to give without getting. As the famous "love chapter" of the Bible says, "Love never fails."[6]

How can this be? Is anything really fail proof? Well, at

whatever point you are feeling weak, you can garner every ounce of strength in the room by emptying yourself of the burden to get your own way. That never fails. Truly.

> `There is a calmness to a life lived in gratitude, a quiet joy.
>
> RALPH H. BLUM

Recently, I received a heated e-mail from a colleague at my university who had jumped to an irrational conclusion about the way I administered exams and assigned grades in one of my classes. Among other things, she accused me of having our office staff grade student papers for me, a definite no-no in academic circles and, further, something that wouldn't even enter my mind.

Although my colleague's accusation was erroneous, it didn't stop her from launching into an in-person tirade against me. I was shocked, not only by the boldness and irrationality of her accusations, but also by her personal attack on my character. In fact, I was livid. *Where does this person get off on making outlandish accusations about me without even checking with me first?* Everything within me was gearing up to push back. But I didn't. I made a decision to set my ego aside, as best I could, and extend grace to my accuser.

"Molly," I said, gently and with honest concern, "where's this anger coming from?" That was it. In that moment of genuine compassion, I was free. In that moment—the second she could see my grace-filled spirit—I stood strong. It wasn't a technique or a maneuver. I truly emptied myself of me. I let go of my defenses. I let go of my desire to set her straight. Now, I guarantee that if I had launched back at her with equally cruel comments, the relationship would have been in turmoil. I would have obsessed about it, recounting what I could or should have said differently. I would have lost sleep. Most of all, I would have lost the power to be the kind of person I want to be. In the end, my emptiness healed the breach her accusation had caused. We've moved beyond it without further incident.

When you consciously choose a course of action that accents the good of others, a deep change occurs in your soul. Pretentious egoism fades, and your days are punctuated with spontaneous breathings of compassion and generosity, kindness and nurturance. The noblest of human qualities become your new compass. And you will never feel stronger than when you give grace.

But how do you do this with any semblance of consistency?

> A proud man is seldom a grateful man, for he never thinks he gets as much as he deserves.
>
> HENRY WARD BEECHER

THE NOT-SO-GOOD SAMARITAN

If there is anything better than being loved, it is loving. But let's be honest: We love within limits. In the vulnerable process of owning our own weakness (as we saw in chapter 3), we realize that we have needs, drives, rights, and goals that do not easily harmonize with selfless love.[7]

But does that mean that to be emptied we must give up those needs, drives, rights, and goals? I want to be clear: The love that comes from being emptied of self-seeking ways is not necessarily related to self-denial. I have seen many well-intentioned people set out to "love" others by denying their own needs—as if performing a sacrifice were the goal. Not so. Being emptied of self-seeking desires is not the same as doing without. As the greatest of love poems makes clear, we can give our bodies to be burned and still not be loving.[8] Self-giving love does not demand a huge sacrifice. Small things done with great love most often characterize the actions of people who have found the power of surrender. But sometimes, we must admit that even the smallest of sacrifices is hard to come by.

Consider the parable of the Good Samaritan.[9] There is hardly a more famous story of being emptied of self-absorption than this.

The very phrase "Good Samaritan" has been enshrined in our culture by its use in the names of hospitals and care centers worldwide. It's a story that's told and retold in classes and sermons every week. It is one of those passages, like the Christmas and Easter stories, that probably wear out professional preachers because its point seems obvious: It is better to be kind, to take care of a person in need, than to pass by and let him suffer. Enough said.

Or is it?

Princeton University psychologists John Darley and Daniel Batson conducted a landmark study years ago that is now recounted in nearly every university course on social psychology. I've lectured and written on it myself, but it bears repeating. Here's what happened: The researchers met with a group of seminarians individually and asked each to prepare a short, extemporaneous talk and then walk to a nearby building on the campus to present it. Along the way to give their talks, the individual students came upon a man set up by the researchers. Slumped over, head down, eyes closed, coughing and groaning, he was in obvious need of help. The question was, who would stop and lend a hand?

> **Grace isn't a little prayer you chant before receiving a meal. It's a way to live.**
>
> JACKIE WINDSPEAR

To highlight the results, Darley and Batson introduced some variables. For example, they varied the topic the students were to talk on. Some were asked to speak on their vocations as members of the clergy. Others were assigned the parable of the Good Samaritan. In addition, for some students, the experimenter would look at his watch and say, "Oh, you're late. They were expecting you a few minutes ago. We'd better get moving." In other cases, he would say, "It will be a few minutes before they're ready for you, but you might as well head over now."

Now, which of these seminary students do you think were

most likely to stop to help the man in need? If you're like most people, you would say that those who had just read the parable of the Good Samaritan would be most likely to stop and help. Almost everyone says that. But they are wrong. In fact, having just read the story made almost no difference in the subjects' responses. "It is hard to think of a context in which norms concerning helping those in distress are more salient than for a person thinking about the Good Samaritan, and yet it did not significantly increase helping behavior," Darley and Batson concluded. "Indeed, on several occasions, a seminary student going to give his talk on the parable of the Good Samaritan literally stepped over the victim as he hurried on his way."[10]

> He is a wise man who does not grieve for the things which he has not, but rejoices for those which he has.
>
> EPICTETUS

We all struggle to set aside self-interest and let go of our personal agendas. Pride, not to mention our schedules, seems to continually interfere with our loving efforts. And when you add some personal pain to our prideful nature, it seems to make the choice of being emptied doubly hard.

SURRENDERING EVEN WHEN PAIN IS PART OF YOUR PICTURE

It is one thing to be emptied of self-centered ways and put up with inconvenience in order to extend some grace to those who might not deserve it. But when your self-centered ways are holding tightly to a life that shouldn't involve pain and you're contending with cancer or an unfaithful spouse, for example, it takes the challenge of surrender to a whole new level.

Of course, all of us hold on to this ideal: Life shouldn't be painful. But it is—for everyone. Nobody is exempt from pain. So if you are carrying personal pain right now as you read these words, I want to help you address this issue head-on, because although you may not believe it, you are stronger than you think. You can surrender what you're holding on to and find a power in your pain. It comes down to choice.

We all know people who have become much meaner and more irritable and more intolerable to live with because they held on to the suffering they've endured. And we've seen people who have been through similar suffering and seem to let go, rise above it, and find healing that engenders an attitude that draws others to them. How could the same suffering produce such different demeanors? Are some people lucky or blessed while others are cursed?

Some people will never get beyond their pain. It will wreak havoc in their personal and professional lives because they will keep cursing their pain—and it will keep cursing them back. They will hold on to it in one of two ways. They will either give in to it with a self-loathing that ensures perpetual misery and failure. Or they will wage an angry and desperate war against it in an effort to bury its devastation in self-denial. Either way, they will never surrender. They will hold on to the idea that their lives shouldn't have pain—that life should be fair. And they will therefore miss out on the power that could be theirs.

> You will find as you look back upon your life that the moments when you have really lived are the moments when you have done things in the spirit of love.
>
> HENRY DRUMMOND

Others, those who choose a higher path, will eventually rise above their pain—not by cursing it but, in an almost incomprehensible twist, by embracing it. They will face the truth of their pain, avoiding the temptation to ignore or deny it. In turn, they will be blessed by it. They will begin to uncover the power that comes from letting go of what their pain is preventing—the life they dreamed of. All because they made the choice to make the best of it while they were getting the worst of it. In other words, they made a choice to be emptied.

But let's be honest. This can sound flip. The choice I'm talking about isn't easy. The ability to make this choice calls upon an inner resource you may not even know you have. This choice demands that you summon your will to do what you think you can't. It requires resolve that can be found only deep in your soul. But this choice does nothing less than determine your destiny.

Your healing hangs on the hinge of this life-changing choice. It's the choice to surrender your desire to have life go the way you planned it. Simply put, it is the choice to find strength in your struggle. It is the choice to find hope in your hurt. It is the choice to choose the direction of your life and the demeanor of your spirit. In short, it is the determination to make the best of the worst.

And sometimes, if you're kicking and screaming against your pain, that seems nearly impossible.

IF YOU FEEL YOU CAN'T MAKE THE CHOICE

If you're like a lot of people, you may want to ask, "What if you simply can't seem to make this choice? What if you don't have the strength?"

If you were to look me in the eye and ask what to do if you just can't make the choice to empty yourself, I would gently say that you're not quite understanding the choice. At this stage, I am simply asking you to lower your defenses and open yourself up to *the idea* of being emptied. That's all. The choice is to open up your spirit and be willing to find a better way through your pain.

> The thankful heart sweeps through the day and, as the magnet finds the iron, so it will find, in every hour, some heavenly blessings!
>
> HENRY WARD BEECHER

And in case you're wondering if you might be an exception to the general rule, you're not. *Everyone can make this choice.* There are countless testimonies to this fact, over the entire span of human history. It is the dividing line between those who rise above their difficulties and those who never recover from hardship and forever suffer its damages. It's not chance. It's choice.

You've probably heard someone say that life is 10 percent what happens to you and 90 percent how you respond to it. Do you agree? It's a tough pill to swallow if you aren't finding the inner strength to rise above your hardship. But I would like to suggest that it takes just as much energy to resist the choice as it does to make it. Resisting the choice may seem less difficult, but it invariably means more work, more pain, and more hardship.

Consider one of the twentieth century's best-known artists, jazz great Duke Ellington. He and his orchestra toured the United States during a period of strident racial discrimination. When he was asked about his feelings at not being able, as a black man, to stay in the guest rooms of the hotels he and his band performed in because of segregation, he said, "I took the energy it takes to pout and wrote some blues."[11]

I'm asking you to do the same. Take the energy it takes to stay stuck in your suffering and use it to write a new chapter in your life. It may not be the one you imagined when you dreamed about your days on this planet, but here you are, and your life story does not have to be dictated by your hardship. You, not your struggles, are the one who will determine what takes place in this next chapter of your life.

If you are a spiritual person, you already know that making this choice is nearly impossible if you think you can muster it on your own. Sure, it requires your will, as I've said. But your will may not be strong enough. That's when you need to ask God to empower you in this effort. Think of it this way: You have an electric power strip with multiple outlets (the kind that computers are plugged into), and you plug various lamps or appliances into it. You would not then plug the power strip into itself and attempt to turn on the lights and appliances. You'd obviously need to plug it into an outlet to receive power. The same is true when it comes to making this choice. If you want to make it but you're not finding the power within you, ask God to infuse you with the strength to do so. As they say in AA, "Let go, and let God."

THE SURE SIGN OF SURRENDER

If you are serious about letting go of the burden of having every-thing go your way—whether you're contending with a deep wound or not—there is a derivative you can anticipate. In fact, it's more than an effect. It's also a cause. That is, it's a clear sign of surrender, but it's also a catalyst for being emptied even further. If you're thinking of grace, you're right, of course, but I've already touched on that. What I'm talking about here is a close cousin of grace—it's gratitude. "Grace and gratitude," said Karl Barth, "go together like heaven and earth."[12]

Scientists are latecomers to the concept of gratitude. Research psychologists have tended to look down their noses at gratitude as little more than a question of having good manners and

> **Grace and gratitude go together like heaven and earth.**
>
> KARL BARTH

remembering to say thank you. In fact, gratitude isn't even listed in the *Encyclopedia of Human Emotions*, a standard psychology text. Experts are saying that gratitude has become the "forgotten factor" in social science research.[13]

But that's changing. New gratitude experiments by social scientists seem to be popping up on university campuses. It seems they're finally embracing what others have been teaching for centuries: that gratitude is an indispensable demonstration of virtue and an integral component to living strong. Why? Because they're seeing how essential gratitude is to joyful surrender.

Scientists are just now beginning to understand what theologian Karl Barth meant when he said, "Joy is the simplest form of gratitude," and what English minister John Henry Jowett said: "Gratitude is a vaccine, an antitoxin, and an antiseptic." Researchers are finding that, indeed, gratitude guards us against gloom. "I'm too blessed to be depressed," as trite and simplistic as it sounds, is more than just a quip on a plaque or a bumper sticker. It's true. Counting your blessings keeps sadness at bay and heightens a positive outlook.

> **To speak gratitude is courteous and pleasant, to enact gratitude is generous and noble, but to live gratitude is a touch of Heaven.**
>
> JOHANNES A. GAERTNER

After all, it's tough to imagine someone saying, "I am so blessed, but I feel miserable."

And that's the payoff of a surrendered soul. Grateful people, researchers are learning, are not those who take a Pollyanna-ish view of the world. In studies, people who score highly on various indicators of gratefulness also report strong awareness of the bad things in their own lives and in society. In fact, some research finds that grateful people may be slightly more likely to be cynical than the population as a whole. But they achieve the ability to be wary of life's problems and yet thankful for the ways in which the actions of others lighten their burdens.

Gratitude reaches down into our very souls and awakens the slumbering feelings of grace and love we have for one another. "If you concentrate on finding whatever is good in every situation," says Rabbi Harold Kushner, "you will discover that your life will suddenly be filled with gratitude, a feeling that nurtures the soul."

THE STRENGTH OF SURRENDER

Remember my friend Bill from an earlier chapter? He told me that the day he left San Quentin, he was a changed man. Bill had just endured the most difficult two and a half years of his life, and he was not the same person he had been when he entered prison. Bill was better.

Gone were the homes, the cars, the money, and the career. He had lost everything—even most of his relationships. Bill's dreams for the way his life was supposed to go had also evaporated. Yet inexplicably, locked in a prison cell, Bill was complete and feeling stronger than he ever had before. How could that be?

When Bill had first entered San Quentin, he told me, his focus was on everything he had lost. He could see only in reverse, lamenting every poor choice, reliving every regret. Bill couldn't see how life would or could ever be good again. His dreams were dashed against the cold reality of San Quentin. Bill saw nothing but impossibilities and no hope. He was truly imprisoned—in body, mind, and soul.

But during his prison experience, something changed. Even though he had lost everything, he hadn't let go. Like the monkey holding tightly to the banana, Bill had a vise grip on what he thought his life was about and what was supposed to make him happy. And because of the clenched fist around Bill's past and what was supposed to be his future, Bill was in greater internal bondage than any physical prison could put him in. But if he wanted to be free—truly free—he needed to let go. Bill needed to surrender all of it: the past, the future, and whatever would come in the present.

> I have learned how to be content with whatever I have.
>
> PHILIPPIANS 4:11

Bill told me that one day, about a year before his release, he had determined to do just that. Bill decided to let go, mentally, emotionally, and spiritually. And the moment he did, he released the burden of having to make his life go the way he thought it should. Bill released the burden of having to get his own way.

This was a dividing line in his life, and it was marked by freedom. Not physical freedom—it happened a year before he walked out of prison. It was a freedom that had nothing to do with incarceration; it had to do with freedom of the soul.

Bill's newfound freedom brought a level of gratitude he had never experienced before. He was holding tightly to nothing except a genuine thankfulness for "today"—whatever it might hold.

FOR REFLECTION

1. What parts of your will are you holding most tightly? In other words, what desires are the toughest to release? How would your spirit be different if you were to ease your grip and let them go?

2. Do you agree that love is the ultimate power? Do you view being emptied of yourself as a means to making room in your soul for love? How does this look, at a practical level, in your daily life?

3. What do you make of the Good Samaritan study, in which some students didn't stop to help, even though they valued this kind of compassion? How do you think you would have behaved if you were one of the subjects of the study? Why?

4. Would you say your level of gratitude for "today" is deep and genuine? How would you rate it and why? Is it deep enough to be genuinely thankful even in the dark days of your life?

WORKBOOK EXERCISE 5

If you are using the optional workbook, the exercise for this chapter will reveal the parts of your life you are clutching most tightly. It will show you how loosening your grip and letting go in these areas can bring you new strength. Most important, it will show you how to release the burden of having to make everything in your life go the way you want it to. And it will walk you down the path to a deep and abiding gratitude that is resting within your soul.

Be Emptied

6

BE BOLD
THERE'S STRENGTH IN TAKING RISKS

Faith is the daring of the soul
to go farther than it can see.
—William Newton Clarke

Why do some people lose courage while others look for solutions? Why do some play it safe while others take risks? Why do some give up and remain passive while others overcome obstacles and achieve results?

Martin Seligman stumbled onto the answer when he was just twenty-one years old. It was his first year of graduate school in psychology in the 1970s when, thanks to B. F. Skinner, "behaviorism" was all the rage among novice researchers. Animals were being conditioned to do everything from ringing a bell to playing Ping-Pong.

So Seligman and his associates conducted an experiment in which dogs were learning to associate a tone with a very mild shock, akin to static electricity. The dogs were restrained in a harness and then repeatedly exposed to the sound, followed by the shock. The hypothesis was that later, upon hearing the same tone, the conditioned dogs would associate it with an oncoming shock and run or otherwise try to escape.

But what happened next was not expected.

Seligman placed an unrestrained dog inside a shuttle box, a container divided in half by a low wall. When the tone sounded, the dog could easily escape the discomfort of the mild shock by jumping over the wall into the other half of the box. But the researchers were stunned by the dog's response.

On hearing the tone, the dog lay down and began to whine instead of jumping to the other side of the box. How could this be? Even when the shock came, the dog did nothing to evade it. A full two-thirds of the dogs in this experiment didn't even try to escape the negative stimulus.

> To one who has faith, no explanation is necessary. To one without faith, no explanation is possible.
>
> THOMAS AQUINAS

Seligman concluded that these dogs had "learned" to be helpless. In the early conditioning, they had received a shock no matter how much they barked or jumped or struggled; they learned that nothing they did mattered.[1] Why try if you feel you can't win?

Have you ever felt like one of those dogs? Have you ever been tempted to give up because it seemed as if very little you did mattered? If so, you're not alone.

Everyone, at some point, becomes like the dogs in Seligman's experiment. We all respond in a helpless manner on occasion because our experiences have taught us that in ourselves, we are not as strong, not as powerful, as we thought we were. In our attempts to achieve goals, fulfill dreams, or overcome hardships and obstacles, we were thwarted. As a result, our confidence was shaken, our faith became fractured, and we put the adventure of our lives on hold.

But no longer. I hope this chapter becomes a bit of a pivot

point in your life. Whether you've put your life on hold because of a deferred hope (a dream that's been in abeyance) or a dashed hope (a dream that was derailed through no choice of your own), I want to clear the way for a bold step that will leverage the strength you didn't know you had.

LIFE IS NOT A DRESS REHEARSAL

Some people think being bold is being stupid, like "fire walking" across hot coals in your bare feet. But that's not what I'm talking about. This has nothing to do with skydiving or bungee jumping, either. In fact, it has nothing to do with adrenaline or thrill seeking. For our purposes, being bold means living life to the fullest. It's about transcending learned helplessness and living a strong life powered by passion.

Solomon, the wise king, spent years of his life searching for passion. In chapter 9 of Ecclesiastes, the chronicle of that search, Solomon wrote, "Whatever you do, do well. For when you go to the grave, there will be no work or planning or knowledge or wisdom."[2] People read that and think Solomon is saying, "Eat, drink, and be merry, for tomorrow you may die," but that's not it at all. He's saying, "Throw your whole heart into whatever you do. Live while you have the chance."

Nadine Stair got the message, if only too late. You may not know her name, but you may have heard about something the late Mrs. Stair, of Louisville, Kentucky, said when she was asked, at age eighty-five, what she would do if she had her life to live over

> If you hear a voice within you say, "You cannot paint," then by all means paint, and that voice will be silenced.
>
> VINCENT VAN GOGH

again. She had a memorable answer: "I'd dare to make more mistakes," she said. "I would relax. I would be sillier. I would take fewer things seriously. I would perhaps have more actual troubles and fewer imaginary ones. You see, I'm one of those people who lived seriously and sanely hour after hour, day after day. If I had it to do over again, I would take more chances. I would climb more mountains and swim more rivers."

Nadine went on to say, "If I had to do it over again, I would travel lighter than I have. If I had my life to live over, I would start barefoot earlier in the spring and stay that way later in the fall. I would go to more dances. I would ride more merry-go-rounds. I would greet more people."[3]

Do you ever feel as if the days of your life have become too sensible, too sane—too safe? If so, you know that your dreams lie dormant because of too much caution. As the German poet Johann von Schiller said, "The overcautious will accomplish little." In other words, when we are overly cautious, we meander through our days with a malaise that keeps us waiting for our lives to *really* begin. When our lives are too controlled, too cautious, we lose our passion. We lose our strength.

> **Learned helplessness is the giving-up reaction, the quitting response that follows from the belief that whatever you do doesn't matter.**
>
> MARTIN SELIGMAN

Author Eileen Guder puts it a bit more bluntly: "You can live on bland food so as to avoid an ulcer; drink no tea or coffee or other stimulants, in the name of health; go to bed early and stay away from night life; avoid all controversial subjects so as never to give offense; mind your own business and avoid involvement in other people's problems; spend money only on necessities and save all you can. You can still break your neck in the bathtub, and it will serve you right."[4]

Sure, it's a bit callous, but let's admit it: Living boldly, living with power and strength, is not about playing it safe. You may not live on bland food. You may drink plenty of coffee. You may stay up late and be a bit reckless with your money. But that's not the point. Guder's message is directed to all of us who live encumbered with too much caution, never venturing beyond the emotional security of our self-imposed comfort zones.

A DREAM DEFERRED OR A DREAM DASHED?

To figure out what people do in a typical day, interviewers talked to four thousand Americans. Study participants were asked to split up the prior day into fifteen-minute periods and relive what they did, who they were with, and how they felt. These four thousand people were selected to represent every part of the United States, matching census data on age, gender, ethnicity, and so on.

According to the findings, in a typical day we spend just over 17 percent of our time in activities that we find enjoyable and meaningful. That's just twenty-five minutes per day doing what we love: playing with children, listening to music, being in nature, and so on. And the vast majority of us spend nearly 20 percent of every day in unsatisfying activities such as commuting to work or fixing a broken appliance. The rest of our time is spent in the middle, passively accepting whatever the day holds.[5] Clearly, most of us are not waking up in the morning and hollering, "Carpe diem!" We're not living with passion.

Why is that? Two primary reasons—we touched on these in the introduction of this book. First, some of us play it safe. Life is going along okay. We're making it. We've found an easy groove. The problem is that this groove, if we're not mindful, can eventually become a rut. And the longer we stay stuck in it, the less passion we have for living.

A public opinion poll taken by the National Opinion Research Center found that more than half of all adults in their twenties rate their lives as "exciting." Once people reach their forties, this slips to 46 percent. At age sixty it falls to 34 percent. The Nobel Prize–winning French philosopher, physician, and musician Albert Schweitzer fervently believed, "The tragedy of life is what dies inside a person while they live."

That sentiment makes me wince. As the years slide by, far too many of us don't so much live as merely exist. We play it safe, rarely venturing outside our emotional comfort zones. We trade passion for security. Is it a worthwhile trade? I don't think so. As I'm about to show you, I think the strength and power that come from living with passion are worth the risk.

> There is no passion to be found playing small—in settling for a life that is less than the one you are capable of living.
>
> NELSON MANDELA

So if you've been playing it safe—deferring your dream—I hope you'll soon consider taking a bold step. It need not be big, just bold. Why? Because your dream, your true passion, is found just outside the boundary of your comfort zone. It's true for everyone. Dreams are never discovered in safety. They always require risk. Dreams are found and fulfilled in the unknown, in the frightful forest of Big Ideas. Without risking a venture into the unknown, we end up settling for a life we never would have predicted. But that doesn't have to be the case—no matter how far along life's journey we've come and no matter how daunting your dream may seem. Before I'm done, I'll show you how to take that courageous first step.

But first, we have to acknowledge that some of us are not living with as much passion as we'd like, not because we're playing it safe but because we're plagued with pain. Our dreams have been dashed. Our hearts have been broken, we've fallen ill, or we've lost our jobs. Whatever the source, we're contending with hurt or hardship. If this is your situation, you probably could not care less about launching a passionate dream right now. Your concern is just getting through the day. You may feel stuck. Anger, resentment, or maybe apathy and capitulation are creeping in. You may feel like one of Seligman's dogs, and you're tempted to give up on life's dreams. You may be thinking that being bold has little application to your circumstances. But I humbly beg to differ. You, more than anyone else, can find strength in being bold. I dedicate the next section of this chapter specifically to you.

BEING BOLD WHEN YOU'RE FEELING WEAK

Some time ago, boxer Mike Tyson was meeting with reporters before a big title fight. One reporter phrased his question something like this: "Mike, your opponent has been watching films of your other fights. He has a plan to beat you. What are you going to do about that?"

In his signature high-pitched voice and lisp, Tyson said, "Man, everyone's got a plan . . . until they get hit." Chances are you did too. And then you took a sucker punch from life that you never saw coming.

> It is easy to be brave from a safe distance.
>
> AESOP

Everyone gets laid low by illness or hardship or failure sometimes, however briefly. The real difference between people who pull themselves out somehow and the people who do not, says Susan Nolen-Hoeksema, a psychologist at Yale, is that some slip into "rumination"—a spiral of morbid self-involvement that's extremely difficult to shake.[6] But what separates the ruminators from those who are resilient? Why is it that the same set of circumstances that drives one person deeper into the mud makes another stronger?

Studies point to what is known as being emotionally and intellectually "malleable." In chapter 1, I told the story of Josh Waitzkin, the chess prodigy. His teacher, Bruce Pandolfini (played by Ben Kingsley in *Searching for Bobby Fischer*), says chess is a game of failure. "At the beginning, you lose—a lot. The kids who are going to succeed are the ones who learn to stand it." He goes on to say that a lot of young players find losing so devastating that they never adapt, "they never learn to metabolize that failure and to not take it personally. But good players lose and then put the game behind them emotionally."[7]

In other words, Pandolfini teaches his students a calming sense of perspective. He helps them see the big picture and not get so focused on their losses. He teaches them to stop ruminating. The present moment is laid out against the past. He calls it chess instruction, but really, it works with any emotional pain. Studies reveal that teachers who can teach this kind of perspective-taking can foster resiliency among students, creating students who don't flinch from failure but actually welcome it as a learning opportunity. It's not so different from the way writing down your feelings in a journal helps you to process hurt and hardship and then move on.[8]

It was Carol Dweck, a psychologist at Stanford, who identified the dividing line of this capacity as "malleability" in our thinking.[9] That is, when we view our lives as works in progress—whatever happens—we can boldly see that the way forward is up.

It all comes down to treating our hardship, treating our pain, as a teacher and seeing what lessons it has to teach us.

Smooth seas do not make skillful sailors.

AFRICAN PROVERB

Easy to do? Not on your life! That's why it requires boldness. It demands courage. And even in the face of bravery, we will fail. Despite our best intentions, our mightiest resolve, we will find ourselves resisting the lessons our pain and hardship want to teach us. But that's the point. If we can will ourselves to be malleable enough once more, our pain and failure will give us another chance to learn. And if we resist again, they still remain ready to teach us, but only when we are bold enough to hear their lessons.

YOU'RE STRONGER THAN YOU THINK

A BOLD AND DETERMINED SOUL

We meet a lot of people who sigh deeply and say they're looking for their passion, for something to set their souls on fire. But they never find it. Why? Because passion doesn't come from finding it "out there"; passion is an inside job.

Hear this: Passion *does not* produce commitment. *Commitment produces passion.* Once you give yourself to a person or a project, you *become* passionate. It's not the other way around. Your commitment fuels a devotion and a passion that last long after the average person has given up. Artist, scientist, and inventor Leonardo da Vinci possessed unquenchable passion—because of his commitment. "Obstacles cannot crush me," he said. "Every obstacle yields to stern resolve. He who is fixed on a star does not change his mind."

A burning commitment lights the fire of passion. And passion reduces apathy to ashes. American writer Ella Wheeler Wilcox said it nicely in her poem "Will":

> *There is no chance, no destiny, no fate,*
> *Can circumvent or hinder or control*
>   *The firm resolve of a determined soul.*

So where does this determination, this commitment, come from? One thing is certain: It's not born out of reward. Contrary to behaviorist B. F. Skinner's famous theory of positive reinforcement, which suggested that we perform better when we expect to get something out of it, psychologists now see that for long-lasting impact, our behavior must stem from an *intrinsically* rewarding commitment.

James Garbarino, of Loyola University Chicago, asked individual sixth-grade girls to try to teach a new game to a younger child. He promised each girl a free movie ticket if she did a good job. He also asked another group of students if they'd like to try their hand at tutoring, but he said nothing to these girls about a reward. They would be doing it only because they had volunteered to do so.

What Garbarino wanted to know was which group would teach more effectively. He found that those who were after the movie tickets took longer to communicate ideas, got frustrated more easily, and ended up with pupils who didn't understand the game as well as the children who learned it from girls who were not promised a reward. Not only that, but the girls who were teaching without reward viewed the activity as something they would like to continue doing.[10]

As Harvard University social psychologist Teresa Amabile put it, "We look to those extrinsic pressures and say, 'That must be why I'm doing this.'"[11] In other words, we miss out on the mission. The fascination and enthusiasm for the cause mysteriously vanish along the way unless we're motivated by our own personal commitment.

I say it again: *Passion is an inside job.* A burning commitment lights the fire of passion—and a soul on fire is what makes us bold. It's what propels us forward when other people have given up. It's what keeps us going even after failure. It's what moves us ahead in the face of criticism or embarrassment because we continue to listen to the sacred whispers of that still, small voice that calls us to be bold.

> **Freedom lies in being bold.**
> ROBERT FROST

A NEAR-LIFE EXPERIENCE

"Nothing great in the world has been accomplished without passion," said German philosopher Georg W. F. Hegel. The late Steve Jobs was a testimony to that fact. Few would argue against the passion and commitment of the innovative cofounder of Apple and Pixar Animation Studios. So what helped that guy—and helps others like him—fan the fire in his soul? Jobs gave a commencement address at Stanford University that reveals an answer: "Remembering that I'll be dead soon is the most important tool I've ever encountered to help me make the big choices in life. Because almost everything—all external expectations, all pride, all fear of embarrassment or failure—these things just fall away in the face of death, leaving only what is truly important."[12]

That's called perspective. And few things put life into clearer perspective than death. Keeping our mortality in mind is enough for many of us to step outside our comfort zones and boldly embrace life.

THE RISK-TAKER'S ADVANTAGE

Some people never risk taking a bold step because they're waiting for a "lucky break." They think the lives they long for are someday going to fall into their laps. You've no doubt known people who think life will begin once they get a promotion, or find someone to marry, or get out of debt, or whatever. And you have seen that study after study show that those who are extremely happy, those who are living their dreams, usually have the same problems as everyone else, if not more serious ones. So what's the difference between those groups of people? The ones who are living their dreams have discovered the risk-taker's advantage.

> A ship in harbor is safe, but that is not what ships are built for.
>
> PHILANTHROPIST
> JOHN SHEDD

The members of the 1949 class of Harvard Business School were stunningly successful. *Fortune* magazine dubbed them "The Class the Dollars Fell On."[13] When these graduates were in their midfifties, a landmark study revealed that some of them ranked high on a scale of well-being and demonstrated passion for living, while others came in at the bottom of the scale and showed little contentment, let alone passion.

Compared with any other group of Americans of their age, this entire class had done exceptionally well, but some were still soured on life. They suffered from boredom in their work and seemed to feel they could have excelled in their careers even more. Their ego wounds in their business lives spread discontentment to their marriages, their relationships with their children, and their health.

When researchers probed the data to understand the dynamics of these unhappy people, they discovered that much of the class members' despondency was due to a single quality. In fact, it was the most prominent quality separating the two groups. The happiest group from this class had a willingness to risk change; the unhappy group resisted it. Two-thirds of them, in fact, said they would love to change what they do—but they don't. The researchers concluded that "even among men for whom a superior education has opened many doors, well-being is not easily sustained without a continuing willingness to risk change."[14]

> Anything I've ever done that ultimately was worthwhile . . . initially scared me to death.
>
> BETTY BENDER

Don't misunderstand. The advantage is not related to risk takers' being impulsive or careless. It's related to boldness, not bravado. Action, not arrogance. Risk, not recklessness. A calculated risk invigorates the soul and expands one's life. "Man cannot discover new oceans," said French author André Gide, "unless he has the courage to lose sight of the shore."[15]

We all have a shore that gives us security. It represents the comfortable and easy parts of our lives that we know well. What might happen if you had the courage to lose sight of the shoreline that keeps calling you back from discovering new oceans? And what might those oceans be? Only you can answer. And when you do, you're beginning to embody the risk-taker's advantage.

A VERY BOLD RISK

Our dreams—whether deferred or dashed—are specific to us as individuals. Our dreams are like nobody else's, yet we all share at least one big dream that is aflame within the soul of every human: to love. It is a dream that demands boldness like no other, because it is fraught with countless obstacles. It is, in fact, the most challenging act of the human spirit. Yet it is the *summum bonum*, the supreme good. "Take away love," said Robert Browning, "and our earth is a tomb." Without love, no other dreams matter.

One of the best antidotes to overcoming any obstacle on the road to fulfilling this dream was penned in 1968 by Kent Keith, a nineteen-year-old college sophomore. While attending Harvard College, Kent gave more than 150 speeches at high schools, student leadership workshops, and student council conventions. He was providing an alternative student voice during the 1960s, when student activists were staging demonstrations at which they shouted down their opponents, took over buildings, and sometimes threw rocks at police who were trying to keep order. Kent encouraged students to work for change through the system.

But he soon learned that many students didn't know how to work through the system. When things got difficult or the system didn't work fast enough, these students tended to give up: "I saw a lot of idealistic young people go out into the world to do what they thought was right, and good, and true," recalls Keith, "only to come back a short time later, discouraged, or embittered, because they got negative feedback, or nobody appreciated them, or they failed to get the results they had hoped for."

Kent told his fellow students that to change the world, they had to love people—even when it wasn't easy: "The challenge is

> **You must do the thing you think you cannot do.**
>
> ELEANOR ROOSEVELT

to always do what is right and good and true, even if others don't appreciate it."[16]

Pretty impressive words for a college sophomore! But even more impressive is how he summarized his challenge. It came in the form of what he called the "Paradoxical Commandments." If you've heard them before, they're worth reading again. And again.

Here they are:

1. People are illogical, unreasonable, and self-centered. Love them anyway.
2. If you do good, people will accuse you of selfish ulterior motives. Do good anyway.
3. If you are successful, you win false friends and true enemies. Succeed anyway.
4. The good you do today will be forgotten tomorrow. Do good anyway.
5. Honesty and frankness make you vulnerable. Be honest and frank anyway.
6. The biggest men with the biggest ideas can be shot down by the smallest men with the smallest minds. Think big anyway.
7. People favor underdogs, but follow only top dogs. Fight for a few underdogs anyway.
8. What you spend years building may be destroyed overnight. Build anyway.
9. People really need help but may attack you if you do help them. Help people anyway.
10. Give the world the best you have and you'll get kicked in the teeth. Give the world the best you have anyway. [17]

Today, Kent Keith continues to proclaim the message of these Paradoxical Commandments as a speaker and writer, and his powerful list has been spread far and wide—and often not attributed to him. In fact, you may find Mother Teresa's name attached to those words. But she didn't write them. Kent did.

Why the misplaced attribution? Most likely because Mother Teresa put them on the wall of her children's home in Calcutta. Imagine that. Even Mother Teresa, the icon of a bold dreamer of love, must have found it difficult to live in line with those commandments on occasion.

Yet she did so anyway.

BOLD LOVE

Mother Teresa was a risk taker. She embodied boldness. As a result, the diminutive nun in Calcutta, India, found strength in her soul she didn't even know she had. And that's the point. Be bold, because there is strength in taking risks—especially when those risks revolve around love.

Victoria Ruvolo, of Lake Ronkonkoma, New York, illustrates the point like few others. She had every reason to harbor hate. But she didn't. She loved anyway.

One wintry night, Victoria was driving to her niece's voice recital when she passed another car driven by nineteen-year-old Ryan Cushing. Cushing was riding with five other teens and had just come from a spending spree in which he used a stolen credit card. One of his purchases was a frozen turkey, which Cushing decided to toss into oncoming traffic. The twenty-pound projectile smashed through Victoria's windshield, crushing her face, shattering the socket of her left eye, and rendering her unconscious.

Amazingly, Victoria survived, although she spent ten hours in an operating room while doctors repaired her face. When she finally went home, she had a tracheotomy tube and endured months of painful rehabilitation.

When Victoria attended Cushing's sentencing for his crime, she asked the presiding judge for leniency. Her statement read, in part, "Despite all the fear and the pain, I have learned from this horrific experience, and I have much to be thankful for. . . . Each day when I wake up, I thank God simply because I'm alive. I sincerely hope you have also learned from this awful experience, Ryan. There is no room for vengeance in my life, and I do not believe a long, hard prison term would do you, me, or society any good."

> Permanence, persever- ance, and persistence in spite of all obstacles, discouragement, and impossibilities: It is this, that in all things distinguishes the strong soul from the weak.
>
> THOMAS CARLYLE

Cushing, who wept in her arms during a court appearance after handing Victoria a handwritten, four-page apology, expressed remorse for his senseless action. He was sentenced to six months in jail. He had faced up to twenty-five years on multiple felony charges, and that's what he would have received if Victoria, his victim, had not intervened.

Victoria added, "I truly hope that by demonstrating compassion and leniency I have encouraged you to seek an honorable life. If my generosity will help you mature into a responsible, honest man whose graciousness is a source of pride to your loved ones and your community, then I will be truly gratified, and my suffering will not have been in vain. . . . Ryan, prove me right."[18]

Victoria Ruvolo is a risk taker. She believes in being bold.

What is remarkable is that Victoria does not regret insisting that the district attorney press only the lightest of charges against Mr. Cushing for hurling the turkey that, had her companion in the passenger seat not grabbed the mangled steering wheel and pulled the car off the road, might have been a death weapon.

This was not the first loss Victoria experienced. In fact, she has suffered more than her share of losses. When she was thirteen, she watched as an older brother was carried from their home in a body bag after an accidental overdose. When she was seventeen, another brother died in a car accident. Her brother-in-law was murdered when Victoria was twenty-one. At thirty-five, and eight months pregnant, she miscarried the baby girl she had named Christina.

> Faith is the daring of the soul to go farther than it can see.
>
> WILLIAM NEWTON CLARKE

Victoria knows the pain of dashed dreams. She also knows the inexplicable strength of bold love.

THE FIRST STEP IS THE HARDEST

"A journey of a thousand miles begins with a single step." As clichés go, that's pretty wise. After all, being bold can sound scary, because being bold leads to the unknown. It requires a willingness to risk change. And everyone fears change. That fear is rooted deep in our brains' physiology. That's why before we leave this chapter, I've got to make this important point: *Being bold does not require a "leap of faith." It asks only that you take the first step.*

Inertia is the enemy of boldness. It causes us to wait for "someday." To wait for the time when the conditions are perfect, or when everyone agrees with us. It looks for any reason to avoid being bold. The only cure for the inertia of waiting on "someday" is to take a small step now. Martin Luther King Jr. may have said it best: "Faith is taking the first step even when you don't see the whole staircase."

What does that first step look like for you? And what's keeping you from taking it? I pray you won't lie helpless like the dogs in the shuttle box of Martin Seligman's experiment. One small step was all that was required for those discontented dogs to find freedom.

Dr. Seligman wrote his first paper on the phenomenon of learned helplessness shortly after earning his PhD in 1967. He spent the rest of his life exploring it. I had the good fortune of sharing a meal with Dr. Seligman some time ago in Monterey, California, and he told me it still amazes him that some people react just like the majority of the dogs in his laboratory when exposed to an obstacle or a challenge. Some people give in to helplessness, fearing they don't have what it takes to succeed or realize their dreams. Others show a bold and unflinching determination to find a way through tough times. Their commitment enflames their passion, and their passion moves them toward their dreams.

> If you want to walk on water, you've got to get out of the boat.
>
> JOHN ORTBERG

The difference between those two groups is the inclination to take a bold step and discover the strength that comes in taking risks.

FOR REFLECTION

1. Do you consider yourself to be a bold person? Why or why not? When you hear the word *bold*, what feelings come to mind? Are they positive or negative?

2. On a scale of 1 to 10, how would you rate at throwing yourself into your own life? Are you living with passion, or have your days become a bit mundane? What are some specific examples that demonstrate your assessment?

3. Can you think of a time in your life when you lived out bold love? a time when you loved anyway or did good anyway?

4. What is one small step you could take today that would demonstrate your boldness? What's the risk involved in taking that step?

WORKBOOK EXERCISE 6

If you are using the optional workbook, the exercise for this chapter will help you find the places in your life in which inertia is winning over your desire to be bold. More important, it will show you how to find the fire in your soul, where passion resides, and how to leverage it to realize your dreams.

MAKING IT REAL
LEVERAGING THE POWER OF YOUR SOUL

True religion is real living: living with all one's soul.
—ALBERT EINSTEIN

Now that you have read these two chapters devoted to the power of the soul, you might be tempted to simply absorb what you've read, to ponder it. But merely thinking about it would do little to get you to the point of summoning the strength it offers. That's why I want to help you put it into action. "A little knowledge that acts," said Kahlil Gibran, "is worth infinitely more than much knowledge that is idle."

So how are you doing when it comes to finding strength deep down in your soul? If you're like most people, the soul may be the most challenging place from which to leverage your untapped power. It is the area that requires you to dig deepest—to literally search your soul. So I ask again, how are you doing here? How does what you've just read apply to you and your life?

If your dreams have been derailed and dashed by pain or

hardship, it is likely to be the power you find in your soul that gets you back on track. And if your dreams have been inadvertently postponed because life seemed to start passing you by, the power you find in your soul is likely to be your saving grace, quite literally.

ARE YOU USING THE POWER OF YOUR SOUL?

As in the previous two sections, I provide you with a brief assessment for heightening your self-awareness. Use it to personalize the information you've read in these last two chapters and to apply the practical helps you will find here. Again, this simple questionnaire is just ten items.

Take your time, and be honest as you consider your responses. There are no right or wrong answers. Just answer yes, no, or maybe to each.

1. I tend to hold tightly to my desires.
   Yes ____ No ____ Maybe ____

2. I often feel helpless, as if little I do really matters.
   Yes ____ No ____ Maybe ____

3. My happiness is too often tied to getting what I want.
   Yes ____ No ____ Maybe ____

4. In general, people would describe my life more as reserved than as bold.
   Yes ____ No ____ Maybe ____

5. I rarely know the freedom that comes from helping others.
   Yes ____ No ____ Maybe ____

6. If I don't change something, I fear that I will have regrets at the end of my life.
   Yes ____ No ____ Maybe ____

7. I tend to focus more on my own needs than on other people's.
   Yes ____ No ____ Maybe ____

8. My life lacks passion.
   Yes ____ No ____ Maybe ____

9. I wish that I felt more genuine gratitude in my life.
   Yes ____ No ____ Maybe ____

10. The fear of taking a risk in order to fulfill my dream often keeps me stuck.
    Yes ____ No ____ Maybe ____

MAKING SENSE OF YOUR RESULTS

Give yourself 2 for every yes, 0 for every no, and 1 for every maybe. Your score will fall somewhere between 0 and 20 points.

If you scored *between 15 and 20*, you can significantly improve the power of your soul. Although you may be feeling quite powerless now, you will see dramatic advances in your sense of well-being when you apply the principles you've learned in this section of the book. There's no need to feel overwhelmed. Taking a few small action steps, noted on the pages that follow, will set you on the right path to leveraging the power of your soul—even if you are not optimistic.

If you scored *between 6 and 14*, you are likely to vacillate between leveraging the power of your soul and overlooking it. That is, sometimes you find great strength because you are leaning into your capacity to be emptied, while at other times you are holding tight to your own desires and personal agenda. In the same way, you can sometimes be bold and courageous, while at other times you tend to be a bit cowardly and overly cautious. You will want to pay special attention to the practical helps that follow in order to more consistently harness the power that comes from being emptied and being bold.

If you scored *between 0 and 5*, your soul is in prime condition to leverage the power that comes from being emptied and being bold. Take advantage of the practical applications that follow to hone your soul's strength. In fact, you'll find a suggestion, specifically for you, for doing just that.

GETTING PERSONAL

I now turn to a few practical suggestions for applying what you have learned in part 3 of this book. As always, view the following suggestions as items on a menu, and focus on those you believe will give you the most beneficial results.

LEVERAGING THE POWER OF BEING EMPTIED

In chapter 5 you saw how personal strength is found when you are emptied—how you can find strength in surrender. Here are a few practical ways of making this real in your own life.

◆ Release Your Burden

This chapter pointed to the weight we all carry in needing to get our own way—how we hold on to aspects of our lives with clenched fists. The question is, in what specific ways are you "demanding" that life go the way you want it to go? Does something readily come to mind? If not, give it some thought. Nearly everyone is holding tight to a personal agenda of some kind. It could relate to what you want your child to do or how you want your spouse to behave. It could be about what should happen in your career or what doors should be opened for you. It may be about what a friend should be doing. Keep in mind that these are not moral or ethical issues. They are about your *personal* agenda, plan, or desire. I recommend that once you identify one or two of these desires, you consider three things: First, why are you holding on to this agenda so tightly? What's the reason or goal behind it, and what does it do for you? Second, what can you do to loosen your grip on that agenda, and what would that do for your spirit? Be as specific as possible in noting the good and the bad. Finally, put your conclusions into practice. In other words, take a practical step toward letting go of the burden you're carrying to have things go your way.

◆ *Bless Your Pain*

I can almost feel you cringing as you read this. But give me a moment. If you are currently coping with some kind of pain or hardship in your life, this recommendation is just for you. I want you to try letting go of whatever your pain is keeping you from doing or having in the life you dreamed of. How can you possibly do this? By blessing your pain. Now, I know it sounds absurd, but it's a time-tested piece of wisdom that can truly rearrange the particles of your soul. It can help you see your predicament in a light that lets you learn from it instead of being cursed by it. Here's how to make this concrete: Write down the details about what your pain or hardship is causing you to give up (both permanently and temporarily)—the good things you would never choose to miss out on. This ensures that you are embracing the full impact of your loss. Next, make a list of any potential good that you think can or will come out of your current predicament. Be genuine. If you don't believe it, don't put it down. You may find that your list is pretty short. That's okay. The next step is intended to make it a bit longer: Dig down deep in your soul to summon your will to approach your circumstances differently by doing your best to see the bright side of where you are. Why would you do this? Because this process ultimately hinges on your choice to do just that. You're going to need some help, so enroll some friends who will be there to encourage you in ways that are truly helpful (you may need to spell out to them what will work best for you, because everyone is different). And you may find it helpful to have some tangible reminders of the choice you've made. For example, posting a Bible verse or a wise saying in a place where you will see it frequently can be a catalyst for blessing your pain. You are making a big choice, one that will call upon all your emotional and spiritual resources. You'll need to pull out all the stops to make the best of the worst. But it may literally be the best decision you ever make. As I said in chapter 5, this choice does nothing less than determine your destiny.

◆ Start a Gratitude Journal

I talked about how a sense of genuine thankfulness is the sure sign of surrender. We become more conscious of our blessings when we are being emptied. I also pointed to research that found how daily gratitude results in a bundle of positive results. In fact, counting our blessings is one of the easiest and most beneficial exercises we humans can do. So here's my suggestion: Take a moment at the end of each day, just before you fall asleep, to record a couple of things you are particularly grateful for. You've probably heard of doing this in a journal. But you can do it on note cards or a simple sheet of paper you keep by your bed. There is no right or wrong way to do this. The goal is to simply be intentional and cognizant about what you are particularly thankful for. The items can be big, like your health, or small, like the laughter you shared with a friend over lunch. Of course, you can note as many as you want; just don't make the task feel daunting or particularly time-consuming. The idea is to get yourself in the habit of becoming more aware of what makes you appreciative and grateful. You're sure to see and feel the difference deep in your soul. And if you want to take this a step further, you can note at least one person to whom you expressed your gratitude—not a flippant "thanks" but a heartfelt expression of thanks. This will cause you to be more verbal in your appreciation.

LEVERAGING THE POWER OF BEING BOLD

In chapter 6 you saw how being bold and taking risks help you to find personal strength. Here are a few practical ways of doing that.

◆ *Make a Plan for Being Less Helpless*

Chapter 6 began with the research conducted by Martin Seligman and his dogs that learned to be "helpless" when they could have easily changed their unfortunate circumstances—had they only tried. The question is, how have you fallen into the same trap of being helpless when you really were not? More important, what are you doing to practice the opposite of learned helplessness—proactive learned optimism? Let's begin by considering the times or circumstances under which you are most likely to see your-self as helpless. They could be related to a certain family member or something at your job or in your career—anything. Can you put your finger on them? If not, are you willing to ask someone who knows you well to help you out? Once you can identify where you tend to be most "helpless," you can then do something about it. You can outline a course of action that will get you out of your slump in this area. Write down at least one practical action step you can take in the near future to be proactive. Talk it over with a friend to get some objective feedback on your plan, and then set a timeline for implementing it.

◆ Quit Playing It "Safe"

Do you connect with the sentiment of Nadine Stair who, at eighty-five, said that if she had her life to live over again, she would make more mistakes, relax, and be sillier? Most of us want to live lives full of passion, yet we end up working diligently and being overly cautious. We play it safe. What would a passionate life look like for you? In what ways would you be more adventurous, less cautious? What would your life look like if you were traveling lighter and taking fewer things so seriously? Perhaps it would mean being more spontaneous or impulsive. Maybe it would mean splurging a bit more—with either your time or your resources. Perhaps it would simply mean slowing down or saying no to further responsibilities. I want you to think of something you could do—this month—that would "shake things up." What could you do in the next four weeks that you'd be telling your friends about years from now? It doesn't have to be something that requires money. It doesn't even have to require planning. It can just be something you have a whimsy for and you're going to finally do. If nothing comes to mind, by the way, you are probably so "sensible" that you *especially* need to do this exercise. So give it more thought—jot down anything that comes to mind—and do your best to quit playing it so safe.

◆ Do It Anyway

When Kent Keith wrote his ten "Paradoxical Commandments," he was thinking only about his current situation and how to help his fellow students. He had no idea that, years later, they would inspire even Mother Teresa so much that she would have them on her wall to look at frequently. But they did. And they can inspire you, too. I recommend that you review these "commandments" and select one of them that you resonate with most. In other words, which one would you feel best about incorporating into your life—this week: Loving anyway? Being honest anyway? Fighting for an underdog anyway? Next, consider what you will do this week to live out that particular commandment. Try doing this from time to time. Review the list, and lift out the one item that you can practice in the coming days. Write it down. Place it on your desk or on your mirror as a reminder. You will, no doubt, find plenty of reasons not to do it even after you've decided to. But, by all means, do it anyway.

◆ Take a Bold Step

There's a little story about five frogs sitting on a log. Four decide to jump off. How many are left? Answer: five. Why? Because there's a difference between *deciding* to do something and actually *doing* it. That's why in this exercise I am calling you to action. As you know, I encouraged you in this chapter, especially if you have been deferring your dream, to take a bold step. And I said the step need not be big, just bold. This means it needs to be a step that takes you outside your comfort zone. Only you know what that is. Only you know what a risky step in pursuit of your dreams looks like. And only you can take it. So this exercise is brief and to the point: *Take a bold step*. Don't put it off, and by all means, don't simply *decide—do*! Take action. Sure, you need to prepare. So either write down your bold step or tell it to a trusted friend. Give it some thought, and then commit to it. Put it on your calendar. Make a date for your bold step. If it can't be assigned to a specific day for some reason, give it a specified time period. No more procrastinating. It's time to make it happen. It's time to be bold.

CONCLUSION
LET THE ADVENTURE BEGIN

*Life is either a great adventure
or nothing.*
—Helen Keller

George Dantzig was a doctoral student at the University of California at Berkeley in 1939. Arriving late to class one day, he found two problems written on the board. Because he had arrived late, he didn't know they were examples of unproven statistical theorems. Assuming they were a homework assignment, he proceeded to solve them. Years later, as a professor at Stanford, he told what happened next in his own words:

> A few days later I apologized to Neyman [his professor] for taking so long to do the homework—the problems seemed to be a little harder than usual. I asked him if he still wanted it. He told me to throw it on his desk. I did so reluctantly because his desk was covered with such a heap of papers that I feared my homework would be lost there

forever. About six weeks later, one Sunday morning about eight o'clock, [my wife] Anne and I were awakened by someone banging on our front door. It was Neyman. He rushed in with papers in his hand, all excited. "I've just written an introduction for one of your papers. Read it so I can send it out right away for publication." For a minute I had no idea what he was talking about. To make a long story short, the problems on the blackboard that I had solved thinking they were homework were in fact two famous unsolved problems in statistics. That was the first inkling I had that there was anything special about them.

> Dedicate your life to a cause greater than yourself, and your life will become a glorious adventure.
>
> MACK DOUGLAS

A year later, when I began to worry about a thesis topic, Neyman just shrugged and told me to wrap the two problems in a binder and he would accept them as my thesis. . . .

Years later, a friend told Dantzig that he had heard a sermon about him in church, and Dantzig explained how that came about:

The origin of that minister's sermon can be traced to another Lutheran minister. . . . He told me his ideas about thinking positively, and I told him my story about the homework problems and my thesis. A few months later, I received a letter from him asking permission to include my story in a book he was writing. . . . [His] published version was a bit garbled and exaggerated but essentially correct.[1]

Now let me ask you a question: What are the chances that George Dantzig would have continued to try to solve the two problems on the board if he had heard his professor say they had never been solved?

It doesn't matter whether we are told something we are after is impossible or whether we believe it on our own; our natural tendency—once we've drawn the fateful conclusion—is to give up before trying. But George Dantzig learned, without intention, that he was more capable than he had ever imagined.

NOW YOU KNOW

I've done my best in these pages to show you the same thing. You have strength within you that, up to this point, you most likely didn't know you had. A mountain of research backs this up. Countless studies demonstrate how a paradoxical power can be obtained if a person knows where to look:

- In our minds we find power when we clear our heads . . . and when we think expectantly.
- In our hearts we find power when we own our weakness . . . and when we feel connected.
- In our souls we find power when we surrender our egos . . . and when we take bold risks.

That power is ready and waiting. Your adventure is at hand—now, not "someday." If you're living with deferred dreams, it's time to take a step out of whatever is keeping you comfortable and brandish the strength you need to fulfill them. If you're coping with dashed dreams, you can't afford to let your circumstances extinguish your strength. They can serve you now more effectively than at any other point in your life. You don't have to

> An adventure is only an inconvenience rightly considered. An inconvenience is only an adventure wrongly considered.
>
> G. K. CHESTERTON

crack the code of some mysterious combination. You don't have to make a long journey to discover the secret. You hold the power to begin your life's adventure. And you hold it right now. Today.

Dorothy, in *The Wonderful Wizard of Oz*, has had the power to go back to her home in Kansas all along. Her roundabout journey to find the power she is looking for was never necessary. She just didn't know where to find her strength.

But you do. It's found in your mind, your heart, and your soul. To use it—to summon your strength—all you have to do is say you need it and then listen for the still, small voice.

LIVE ALL THE DAYS OF YOUR LIFE

Few stories will stir the human spirit to do just that more than the epic life of one of the world's true heroes: William Wallace. The adventure of his life was popularized in Mel Gibson's Oscar-winning film *Braveheart*. Historians poke holes here and there in the film's accuracy, but nobody disputes the fact that Wallace, a common man, rallied his people in the Scottish Wars of Independence from England by helping them discover strength they never knew they had.[2]

> Here is the test to determine whether your mission on earth is finished: If you're alive, it isn't.
>
> RICHARD BACH

He takes a ragtag band of farmers and villagers to an astounding victory at the battle of Stirling by giving one of the most memorable speeches ever depicted on film: "I am William Wallace. I see a whole army of my countrymen here in defiance of tyranny. You've come to fight as free men, and free men you are. What will you do without freedom? Will you fight?"

One soldier answers, "Against that? No, we will run, and we will live."

"Yes," Wallace replies, "fight, and you may die. Run, and

you'll live . . . at least for a while. And dying in your beds many years from now, would you be willing to trade all the days from this day to that for one chance—just one chance—to come back here and tell our enemies that they can take our lives, but they'll never take our freedom?"[3]

What would you have done, standing among other common villagers, outnumbered by a professional English army? Would you have crept away, trying to go unnoticed, while your countrymen stood strong? I don't believe you would. Like the brave Scots in Wallace's ill-equipped band, you would have rallied to follow him into battle, winning the first major victory of the war and turning the tide against the English.

> **He will keep you strong to the end.**
>
> 1 CORINTHIANS 1:8

And you would have lived without regret.

So why trade the adventure of any of the days you have between now and the time of your death for days that are not lived to the fullest? Your adventure waits on no one but you.

Don't put it off.

Summon your strength to *live* all the days of your life—whatever they may hold—for you *are* stronger than you think.

> ### *I can do all things through Him who strengthens me.*
>
> THE APOSTLE PAUL

NOTES

INTRODUCTION: LIFE IS AN ADVENTURE—IF YOU SUMMON THE STRENGTH

1. "People by Nature Are Universally Optimistic, Study Shows," *ScienceDaily*, May 25, 2009, http://www.sciencedaily.com/releases /2009/05/090524122539.htm. The study, completed by the University of Kansas and presented May 24, 2009, at the annual meeting of the Association for Psychological Science in San Francisco, found optimism to be universal and borderless. Data from the Gallup World Poll drove the findings. The sample included more than 150,000 adults.
2. Edgar A. Guest, "Tomorrow," http://oldpoetry.com/opoem/44730 -Edgar-Albert-Guest-Tomorrow (accessed March 4, 2010).
3. Peggy LeDuff and Nabila Jahchan, "Eggshell Dome Discrepant Event," http://www.csun.edu/~mk411573/discrepant/discrepant_event.html (accessed March 8, 2010). Pressure applied to a dome shape is distributed equally, which gives the dome, in this case an egg, strength to withstand significant pressure from outside itself.
4. When Jesus was asked which commandment was most important, he made no bones about it. It was to love God. But then he explained how to do that: "Love the LORD your God with all your heart, all your soul, all your mind, and all your strength" (Mark 12:30). This passage was the inspiration for the three-part structure of this book, because strength is the outward expression of what is going on within our heads, our hearts, and our souls.
5. Proverbs 13:12.
6. "Hope does not disappoint us, because God has poured out his love into our hearts by the Holy Spirit, whom he has given us" (Romans 5:5, NIV).

PART 1: THE POWER OF YOUR MIND—INTRODUCTION

1. "Even Supercomputers Not Yet Close to the Raw Power of Human Brain," *insideHPC*, March 12, 2009, http://insidehpc.com/2009/03/12 /even-supercomputers-not-yet-close-to-the-raw-power-of-human-brain (accessed March 31, 2010).

2. John Milton, *Paradise Lost*, bk. 1, lines 254–255.
3. Proverbs 27:12.
4. Norman Cousins, *Head First: The Biology of Hope and the Healing Power of the Human Spirit* (New York: Penguin, 1990), 184.

CHAPTER 1: THINK SIMPLY: THERE'S STRENGTH IN CLEARING YOUR HEAD

1. Josh Waitzkin, *The Art of Learning: An Inner Journey to Optimal Performance* (New York: Free Press, 2007), 4.
2. *Searching for Bobby Fischer*, DVD, directed by Steven Zaillian (1993; Hollywood, CA: Paramount Pictures, 2000).
3. Zhenghan Qi and Paul E. Gold, "Intrahippocampal Infusions of Anisomycin Produce Amnesia: Contribution of Increased Release of Norepinephrine, Dopamine, and Acetylcholine," *Learning and Memory* 16 (2009): 308–314.
4. "Chi Chi Rodriguez," an interview by Brent Kelly, *About.com*, http://golf .about.com/od/equipmentreviews/fr/chichigames.htm (accessed February 27, 2010).
5. Michael C. Anderson and Kristin E. Flegal, "Overthinking Skilled Motor Performance: Or Why Those Who Teach Can't Do," *Psychonomic Bulletin and Review* 15, no. 5, http://pbr.psychonomic-journals.org /content/15/5/927.short (accessed February 27, 2010).
6. This is why there have been so many books and publications written over the last thirty years dedicated to helping golfers *stop* thinking. Techniques that cause the golfer to occupy the "thinking part of the brain" have been developed for the purpose of the golfer "letting his body hit the ball." The belief behind this practice is that after the simplest of instruction or practice, the body (in touch with the player's intuition) already knows how to hit the ball. Thinking through the golf swing only complicates the process, thereby leading even the best golfer to struggle with his or her game.
7. Bill Breen, "What's Your Intuition?" *Fast Company*, August 31, 2000, http://www.fastcompany.com/magazine/38/klein.html (accessed February 27, 2010).
8. Gary Klein, *Sources of Power: How People Make Decisions* (Boston: MIT Press, 1998), 2.
9. Thanks to pathways that run from the eye to the brain's emotional-control centers—bypassing the cortex—we often react emotionally before we've even had time to interpret consciously. Below the radar of awareness we can process threatening information in milliseconds. Then, after the cortex has had time to interpret the threat, the thinking brain asserts itself.

10. Gerard P. Hodgkinson, Janice Langan-Fox, and Eugene Sadler-Smith, "Intuition: A Fundamental Bridging Construct in the Behavioural Sciences," *British Journal of Psychology* 99, no. 1 (February 2008): 1–27.

11. Antoine Bechara, "Decision Making, Impulse Control, and Loss of Willpower to Resist Drugs: A Neurocognitive Perspective," *Nature Neuroscience* 8, no. 11 (2005): 1458–63.

12. Romans 12:2 (NIV).

13. Andrew Newberg, MD, and Mark Robert Waldman, *How God Changes Your Brain: Breakthrough Findings from a Leading Neuroscientist* (New York: Ballantine, 2009), 1.

14. John 8:47 (NIV).

15. 1 Corinthians 6:17.

16. Other traditions and cultures have identified this internal phenomenon as well. The ancient Toltec people of Mexico understood it this way: "Your whole mind is a fog which the Toltecs called a *mitote* (pronounced MIH-TOE´-TAY). Your mind is a dream where a thousand people talk at the same time, and nobody understands each other. This is the condition of the human mind—a big *mitote*, and with that big *mitote* you cannot see what you really are." Miguel Ruiz, *Four Agreements: A Practical Guide to Personal Freedom* (Carlsbad, CA: Hay House, 1997), 8.

17. Audrey Barrick, "Survey: Christians Worldwide Too Busy for God," *The Christian Post*, July 30, 2007, www.christianpost.com/article/20070730 /survey-christians-worldwide-too-busy-for-god/index.html (accessed February 27, 2010). The Obstacles to Growth Survey was conducted on 20,000 Christians—the majority of whom came from the United States—from December 2001 to June 2007.

18. Psalm 46:10.

19. "Let the wise listen . . . and become even wiser" (Proverbs 1:5).

20. James 1:5 (NIV).

21. Isaiah 26:3-4.

CHAPTER 2: THINK EXPECTANTLY: THERE'S STRENGTH IN ANTICIPATION

1. Lee Jussim and Kent D. Harber, "Teacher Expectations and Self-fulfilling Prophecies: Knowns and Unknowns, Resolved and Unresolved Controversies," *Personality and Social Psychology Review* 9, no. 2 (2005): 131–55.

2. Robert Rosenthal, PhD, and Lenore Jacobson, PhD, *Pygmalion in the Classroom: Teacher Expectation and Pupils' Intellectual Development* (New York: Irvington, 1992).

3. William Peters, *A Class Divided* (New York: Doubleday, 1971).

4. You've probably heard of this as the "Pygmalion Effect," named after a sculptor in Greek mythology. But it was the musical *My Fair Lady* that artfully demonstrated the power of expectations to Broadway audiences and beyond. See G. K. Chesterton, *George Bernard Shaw* (Oxford: House of Stratus, 1956).

5. This discussion of the impact of self-talk and expectations on our emotions, as well as the following discussion of Mr. Wright and the drug Krebiozen, previously appeared in Les Parrott and Neil Clark Warren, *Love the Life You Live: 3 Secrets to Feeling Good—Deep Down in Your Soul* (Carol Stream, IL: Tyndale, 2004), 38–39.

6. Howard Brody, MD, PhD, *The Placebo Response* (New York: HarperCollins, 2000), 37.

7. Howard Spiro, MD, *The Power of Hope: A Doctor's Perspective* (New Haven, CT: Yale University Press, 1998).

8. Two works that thoroughly document these studies are found in Albert Ellis, *Reason and Emotion in Psychotherapy* (New York: Stuart, 1962) and Aaron T. Beck and others, *Cognitive Therapy of Depression: A Treatment Manual* (New York: Guilford, 1979). In addition, Albert Bandura's article "Self-efficacy: Toward a Unifying Theory of Behavioral Change," *Psychological Review* 84, no. 2 (March 1977): 191–215, greatly strengthened the foundation for this thinking.

9. William James, *The Principles of Psychology* (Cambridge, MA: Harvard University Press, 1983) paperback, 9.

10. Most notably, *The Secret* (Atria Books, 2006) by Rhonda Byrne, an Australian television writer and producer. In fact, *Time* magazine listed her as one of the one hundred people who shape the world. The book has sold more than four million copies.

11. The tenth commandment, found in Exodus 20:17.

12. Deena Winter, "Financial Planners: Winning the Lottery Isn't Always a Dream," February 24, 2006, www.journalstar.com/special-section/news/article_ecba141b-3e59-5914-a321-38b4adb20733.html (accessed February 27, 2010).

13. John Kolligian Jr., *Competence Considered* (New Haven, CT: Yale University Press, 1990), 73.

14. Daniel J. Levinson and others, *Seasons of a Man's Life* (New York: Random House, 1978), 124.

15. Ecclesiastes 1:2.

16. See Romans 5:5.

17. Hebrews 11:1.

18. David Van Biema, "When God Hides His Face," *Time* (July 16, 2001),

http://www.time.com/time/magazine/article/0,9171,1000328,00.html (accessed March 5, 2010).

19. For more of the Guthries' story, see Nancy Guthrie, *Holding On to Hope: A Pathway through Suffering to the Heart of God* (Carol Stream, IL: Tyndale, 2002).

20. Ellen J. Langer and Susan Saegert, "Crowding and Cognitive Control," *Journal of Personality and Social Psychology* 35, no. 3 (March 1977): 175–82.

21. John 16:33.

22. Ibid.

23. Eugene H. Peterson, *A Long Obedience in the Same Direction: Discipleship in an Instant Society* (Downers Grove, IL: InterVarsity, 2000), 144.

24. Lewis Smedes, *Standing on the Promises* (Nashville: Thomas Nelson, 1998).

25. "It is impossible to please God without faith. Anyone who wants to come to him must believe that God exists and that he rewards those who sincerely seek him" (Hebrews 11:6).

26. Matthew 27:46.

27. *A Beautiful Mind,* DVD, directed by Ron Howard (2002; Universal City, CA: Universal Pictures, 2006).

28. Hebrews 13:5.

29. You can read more of Bill's story in his book *Lessons from San Quentin* (Carol Stream, IL: Tyndale, 2009).

PART 2: THE POWER OF YOUR HEART—INTRODUCTION

1. Vijai P. Sharma, PhD, "Heart Is the Seat of Emotions and More," *Mind Publications*, www.mindpub.com/art411.htm (accessed March 11, 2010).

2. Ibid.

3. Ibid.

4. Ibid.

5. Ibid.

6. Matthew 12:34 (NIV).

7. Linda Reid Chassiakos, "Mother-to-be Sacrifices Her Chance of Surviving Cancer for Her Baby," *Los Angeles Times*, May 11, 2009, http://articles.latimes.com/2009/may/11/health/he-practice11.

CHAPTER 3: FEEL VULNERABLE: THERE'S STRENGTH IN OWNING YOUR WEAKNESS

1. C. Randall Colvin, Jack Block, and David C. Funder, "Overly Positive Self-Evaluations and Personality: Negative Implications for Mental

Health," *Journal of Personality and Social Psychology* 68, no. 6 (June 1995): 1152–62.

2. C. Randall Colvin, Jack Block, and David C. Funder, "Psychometric Truths in the Absence of Psychological Meaning," *Journal of Personality and Social Psychology* 70, no. 6 (June 1996): 1252–55.

3. Robert S. Horton and Aiden P. Gregg, "The Why's the Limit: Curtailing Self-Enhancement with Explanatory Introspection," *Journal of Personality* 75, no. 4 (2007): 783–824.

4. According to a comprehensive study by five psychologists, today's college students are more narcissistic and self-centered than their predecessors. From 1982 to 2006, 16,475 college students completed an evaluation called the Narcissistic Personality Inventory (NPI). The standard inventory asks for rated responses to such statements as "If I ruled the world, it would be a better place," "I think I am a special person," and "I can live my life the way I want to." The nationwide results were quite telling. "We need to stop endlessly repeating 'You're special' and having children repeat that back," said the study's leading author, Professor Jean Twenge of San Diego State University. "Kids are self-centered enough already." The study asserts that narcissists "are more likely to have romantic relationships that are short-lived, at risk for infidelity, lack emotional warmth, and to exhibit game-playing, dishonesty, and over-controlling and violent behaviors." The researchers traced the phenomenon back to the self-esteem movement that emerged in the 1980s. See David Crary, "Study: College Students More Narcissistic," Associated Press, February 27, 2007, www.boston.com/news/education /higher/articles/2007/02/27/study_college_students_more_narcissistic (accessed February 28, 2010).

5. Jean M. Twenge, PhD, and W. Keith Campbell, PhD, *The Narcissism Epidemic: Living in the Age of Entitlement* (New York: Free Press, 2009), 15.

6. Diane Mastromarino, *The Girl's Guide to Loving Yourself: A Book about Falling in Love with the One Person Who Matters Most . . . You* (Boulder, CO: Blue Mountain Arts, 2003), 7.

7. Leslie Schenkman Kaplan, "Self-esteem Is Not Our National Wonder Drug," *School Counselor* 42 (1995): 341–45.

8. Twenge and Campbell, *The Narcissism Epidemic*, 116.

9. Stephen Diamond, PhD, "Truth, Lies, and Self-Deception," *Psychology Today*, November 30, 2008, www.psychologytoday.com/blog/evil-deeds /200811/truth-lies-and-self-deception (accessed March 30, 2010).

10. Justin Kruger and David Dunning, "Unskilled and Unaware of It: How Difficulties in Recognizing One's Own Incompetence Lead to Inflated

Self-Assessments," *Journal of Personality and Social Psychology* 77, no. 6 (December 1999): 1121–34.

11. The following books are filled with numerous examples like these: Thomas Gilovich, *How We Know What Isn't So: The Fallibility of Human Reason in Everyday Life* (New York: Free Press, 1993); Herbert Fingarette, *Self-Deception* (Berkeley: University of California Press, 2000); and Alfred R. Mele, *Self-Deception Unmasked* (Princeton, NJ: Princeton University Press, 2001).

12. Tim Urdan, "Predictors of Academic Self-Handicapping and Achievement: Examining Achievement Goals, Classroom Goal Structures, and Culture," *Journal of Educational Psychology* 96, no. 2 (2004): 251–64.

13. Gregg A. Ten Elshof, *I Told Me So: Self-Deception and the Christian Life* (Grand Rapids: Eerdmans, 2009).

14. Robert Harman, "Gestalt Therapy as Brief Therapy," *The Gestalt Journal* 18, no. 2 (1995): 77–85.

15. Thomas Shelley Duval, Paul Silvia, and Neal Lalwani, *Self-Awareness and Causal Attribution* (Norwell, MA: Kluwer, 2001), 1.

16. Daniel Goleman, *Emotional Intelligence: Why It Can Matter More Than IQ* (New York: Bantam, 2006).

17. Peter Salovey and others, "Emotional Attention, Clarity, and Repair: Exploring Emotional Intelligence Using the Trait Meta-Mood Scale," *Emotion, Disclosure, and Health,* ed. James W. Pennebaker, 125–154 (Washington, DC: American Psychological Press, 1995).

18. Daniel Goleman, *Working with Emotional Intelligence* (New York: Bantam, 1998).

19. Proverbs 16:18.

20. Romans 8:15 says, "We should not be like cringing, fearful slaves, but we should behave like God's very own children" (TLB).

21. William Law, a British theologian, put the same sentiment this way: "You can have no greater sign of a confirmed pride than when you think you are humble." In 1621, Robert Burton wrote in *The Anatomy of Melancholy*, "They are proud in humility; proud in that they are not proud."

22. "I tell you the truth, corrupt tax collectors and prostitutes will get into the Kingdom of God before you do," Jesus announced to the religious authorities of his day (Matthew 21:31). After puzzling over that provocative statement, C. S. Lewis concluded, "Prostitutes are in no danger of finding their present life so satisfactory that they cannot turn to God. The proud, the avaricious, the self-righteous, are in that danger."

23. Luke 18:10-14 (*The Message*).

24. Pride is traditionally regarded as the foundational sin. It is understood to be the sin of Satan, expressed in his desire to be like God.

25. Rick Ezell, *The Seven Sins of Highly Defective People* (Grand Rapids: Kregel, 2003), 27–28.

26. 2 Corinthians 12:9.

27. James 4:6 (*The Message*).

28. See Romans 7:18.

CHAPTER 4: FEEL CONNECTED: THERE'S STRENGTH IN BEING KNOWN

1. Richard E. Byrd, *Alone: The Classic Polar Adventure* (Washington, DC: Island Press, 1938), 13.

2. Ibid., 146.

3. Byrd, *Alone*.

4. Ralf Schwarzer and Nina Knoll, "Functional Roles of Social Support within the Stress and Coping Process: A Theoretical and Empirical Overview," *International Journal of Psychology* 42, no. 4 (August 2007): 243–52.

5. John T. Cacioppo and William Patrick, *Loneliness: Human Nature and the Need for Social Connection* (New York: Norton, 2008), 8. The point is that the social pain is more than merely a metaphor.

6. Steve W. Cole and others, "Social Regulation of Gene Expression in Human Leukocytes," *Genome Biology* 8 (2007): R189.

7. Robin I. M. Dunbar and Suzanne Shultz, "Evolution in the Social Brain," *Science* 317 (September 7, 2007): 1344–47.

8. Tori DeAngelis, "A Nation of Hermits: The Loss of Community," *The American Psychological Association Monitor* (September 1995), 45–46.

9. Chip Walker and Elissa Moses, "The Age of Self-Navigation," *American Demographics* (September 1996), 38.

10. David W. Smith, *Men without Friends* (Nashville: Nelson, 1990), 46–47.

11. Shelley E. Taylor, "Social Support," in *Foundations of Health Psychology*, ed. Howard S. Friedman and Roxanne Cohen Silver, 145–71 (New York: Oxford University Press, 2007).

12. We care deeply what others think of us, and that is why, of the ten most common phobias that cause people to seek treatment, three have to do with social anxiety: fear of public speaking, fear of crowds, and fear of meeting new people. Bruskin Associates, "What Are Americans Afraid Of?" *Bruskin Report* 53 (1973): 27.

13. David Buckley, *R.E.M. Fiction: An Alternative Biography* (London: Virgin, 2003).

14. Miller McPherson, Lynn Smith-Lovin, and Matthew E. Brashears,

"Social Isolation in America: Changes in Core Discussion Networks over Two Decades," *American Sociological Review* 71 (June 2006): 353–75.

15. Harvard University study reported in *Harvard Mental Health Newsletter*, February 2008.

16. Although the exact link between chemical imbalance and depression has not been found, clinical studies and medical observations have been able to identify a number of chemical inconsistencies that occur in individuals who report experiencing symptoms related to depression. The most common is a reduction of neurotransmitters such as norepinephrine, serotonin, and dopamine. Collectively, these are known as monoamines, and their loss is what is commonly referred to as a "chemical imbalance."

17. Nina Knoll and others, "Transmission of Depressive Symptoms: A Study with Couples Undergoing Assisted Reproduction Treatment," *European Psychologist* 14, no. 1 (2009), 7–17.

18. At times, social science research may seem like a reality show with a hidden camera that traps unwary people in ridiculous, almost sadistic situations.

19. Rest assured that when experiments like these are completed, the researchers explain all these details to the participants, going to great lengths to ensure that none will come away from the encounter with negative psychological effects.

20. Roy F. Baumeister, Jean M. Twenge, and Christopher K. Nuss, "Effects of Social Exclusion on Cognitive Processes: Anticipated Aloneness Reduces Intelligent Thought," *Journal of Personality and Social Psychology* 83 (2002): 817–27.

21. Roy F. Baumeister and others, "Social Exclusion Impairs Self-regulation," *Journal of Personality and Social Psychology* 88 (2005): 124–34.

22. Nina Knoll and others, "Transmission of Depressive Symptoms."

23. Dov Peretz Elkins, ed., *Glad to Be Me* (Rochester, NY: Growth Associates, 1989), 32.

24. Anne Lamott, *Traveling Mercies: Some Thoughts on Faith* (New York: Anchor, 1999), 213.

25. "Confess your sins to each other and pray for each other so that you may be healed" (James 5:16).

26. C. S. Lewis, *The Four Loves* (Orlando, FL: Harcourt, 1960), 112.

27. William Fry, in his book *Crying: The Mystery of Tears*, suggests that women have an advantage when it comes to crying. Since crying is more socially acceptable for women in our culture, it may enable them the opportunity to excrete their "stress waste" more readily than men, who are conditioned to block this natural cleansing system.

PART 3: THE POWER OF YOUR SOUL—INTRODUCTION

1. "Soul Has Weight, Physician Thinks," *New York Times*, March 11, 1907, http://query.nytimes.com/mem/archive-free/pdf?_r=1&res=9D07E5DC 123EE033A25752C1A9659C946697D6CF (accessed March 12, 2010).

2. Stephen Lemons, "eFaust eFoiled," *Salon*, February 25, 2000, http://www .salon.com/people/log/2000/02/25/soul/index.html.

3. Ken Taylor, "EBay's Idiot Auctions," *Wired*, April 2005, 26, http://www .wired.com/wired/archive/13.04/start.html?pg=5.

4. St. Augustine, *The Greatness of the Soul*, trans. Joseph M. Colleran (New York: Newman Press, 1950), 40.

5. C. S. Lewis, *The Problem of Pain* (New York: HarperCollins, 2001), 152.

6. Harris Interactive, "More Americans Believe in the Devil, Hell, and Angels than in Darwin's Theory of Evolution," *The Harris Poll*, December 10, 2008, http://www.harrisinteractive.com/vault/Harris -Interactive-Poll-Research-Religious-Beliefs-2008-12.pdf.

7. Bradley J. Birzer, author of *J. R. R. Tolkien's Sanctifying Myth: Understanding Middle-Earth*, "Hobbits Aren't Fence-Sitters," *Christianity Today*, December 2002, www.christianitytoday.com/ct/2002 /decemberweb-only/12-16-53.0.html (accessed March 9, 2010).

8. Genesis 2:7 (*The Message*).

9. "Hymn Story of 'It Is Well with My Soul,'" *PreachingToday.com*, http://www.preachingtoday.com/illustrations/search_print.html?type =keyword&query=%22Fruit%20of%20the%20Spirit%22 (accessed March 12, 2010).

CHAPTER 5: BE EMPTIED: THERE'S STRENGTH IN SURRENDER

1. Helmut Thielicke, *How to Believe Again*, trans. H. George Anderson (Philadelphia: Fortress Press, 1972), 27.

2. Bernard B. Rimland, "The Altruism Paradox," *The Southern Psychologist* 2, no. 1 (1982): 8–9.

3. The New Testament's four books on Jesus' life all record his teaching that to *find* our lives, we must be willing to *lose* our lives.

4. Jonathan Haidt, "The Emotional Dog and Its Rational Tail: A Social Intuitionist Approach to Moral Judgment," *Psychological Review*, 108 (2001): 814–34.

5. Martin E. P. Seligman, *Authentic Happiness* (New York: Free Press, 2002), 9.

6. 1 Corinthians 13:8 (NIV).

7. The honest quandary about the tension of self-sacrifice and self-protection has captured many magnificent minds. Anders Nygren's classic book *Agape and Eros* contrasts "acquisitive desire" with "sacrificial

giving." C. S. Lewis called eros "need-love" and agape "gift-love." Thousands of volumes have explored these dueling desires.

8. See 1 Corinthians 13:3.

9. See Luke 10:30-35.

10. John M. Darley and C. Daniel Batson, "From Jerusalem to Jericho: A Study of Situational and Dispositional Variables in Helping Behavior," *Journal of Personality and Social Psychology* 27, no.1 (1973): 100–119.

11. Part 4, *Jazz: A Film by Ken Burns*, DVD, directed by Ken Burns (PBS Home Video, 2001).

12. The word *thanks* and its various cognates (*thankful, thankfulness, thanksgiving*) appear more than 150 times in the Old and New Testaments. The imperative "give thanks" appears thirty-three times.

13. It has been argued that males in particular may resist experiencing and expressing gratefulness, believing that doing so implies dependency and indebtedness. One fascinating study in the 1980s found that American men were less likely to regard gratitude positively than were German men, and to view it as less constructive and useful than their German counterparts. Gratitude presupposes so many judgments about debt and dependency that it is easy to see why supposedly self-reliant Americans would feel queasy about even discussing it.

CHAPTER 6: BE BOLD: THERE'S STRENGTH IN TAKING RISKS

1. Martin E. P. Seligman, *Helplessness: On Depression, Development, and Death* (San Francisco: Freeman, 1975). See also S. F. Maier and Martin E. P. Seligman, "Learned Helplessness: Theory and Evidence," *Journal of Experimental Psychology General* 105 (1976): 2–46.

2. Ecclesiastes 9:10.

3. Nadine Stair, eighty-five-year-old patient of Bernie Siegel, facing death, as quoted in Bernard Siegel, *Peace, Love and Healing: Bodymind Communication and the Path to Self-Healing* (New York: Harper and Row, 1989), 245–46.

4. Eileen Guder, *God, But I'm Bored* (Garden City, NY: Doubleday, 1971).

5. Daniel Kahneman and others, "A Survey Method for Characterizing Daily Life Experience: The Day Reconstruction Method," *Science* 306 (2004): 1776–80.

6. Susan Nolen-Hoeksema, "The Role of Rumination in Depressive Disorders and Mixed Anxiety/Depressive Symptoms, *Journal of Abnormal Psychology* 109 (2000): 504–11.

7. Bruce Pandolfini, *Every Move Must Have a Purpose: Strategies from Chess for Business and Life* (New York: Hyperion, 2003).

8. This phenomenon was demonstrated most clearly by James Pennebaker, PhD, a psychologist at the University of Texas. For more information, see his book *Opening Up: The Healing Power of Expressing Emotion* (New York: Guilford Press, 1990).

9. Carol S. Dweck and Janine Bempechat, "Children's Theories of Intelligence: Implications for Learning," in *Learning and Motivation in the Classroom*, ed. Scott G. Paris, Gary M. Olson, and Harold William Stevenson (Hillsdale, NJ: Erlbaum, no date). See also J. Benenson and Carol S. Dweck, "The Development of Trait Explanations and Self-evaluations in the Academic and Social Domains," *Child Development* 57 (1986): 1179–89; Carol S. Dweck and Lisa A. Sorich, "Mastery-oriented Thinking," in *Coping: The Psychology of What Works*, ed. C. R. Snyder (New York: Oxford University Press, 1999).

10. James M. Cooper, Ellen de Lara, and James Garbarino, *An Educator's Guide to School-Based Interventions* (Florence, KY: Wadsworth, 2003).

11. Teresa M. Amabile and Mukti Khaire, "Creativity and the Role of the Leader," *Harvard Business Review* 86, no. 10 (October 2008).

12. Steve Jobs, commencement address (Stanford University, Stanford, CA: June 12, 2005).

13. Marilyn Wellemeyer, "The Class the Dollars Fell On," *Fortune*, May 1974.

14. Gail Sheehy, *Pathfinders: Overcoming the Crises of Adult Life and Finding Your Own Path to Well-Being* (New York: Morrow, 1981).

15. Risk takers, those who are willing to expand their lives beyond their comfort zones, share a particular discipline worth noting. They listen only selectively to their critics. "You've got to decide sometimes in your life when it's okay not to listen to what other people are saying," says Stacy Allison. She should know. She's the first American woman to reach the summit of Mount Everest. "If I had listened to other people, I wouldn't have climbed Mt. Everest." Quoted in John C. Maxwell, *Put Your Dream to the Test* (Nashville: Nelson, 2009), 149.

16. Kent M. Keith, "The Origin of the Paradoxical Commandments," *Anyway: The Paradoxical Commandments*, http://www.paradoxicalcommandments.com/origin.html (accessed March 2, 2010).

17. Kent M. Keith, *The Silent Revolution: Dynamic Leadership in the Student Council* (Cambridge, MA: Harvard Student Agencies, 1968).

18. Robin Finn, "Pushing Past the Trauma to Forgiveness," *New York Times*, October 28, 2005, http://www.nytimes.com/2005/10/28/nyregion/28lives.html (accessed February 16, 2010).

CONCLUSION: LET THE ADVENTURE BEGIN

1. Donald Albers and Constance Reid, "An Interview with George B. Dantzig: The Father of Linear Programming," *The College of Mathematics Journal* 17 (1986): 301.
2. G. W. S. Barrow, *The Kingdom of the Scots: Government, Church and Society from the Eleventh to the Fourteenth Century*, 2nd ed. (Edinburgh: Edinburgh University Press, 2003).
3. *Braveheart*, DVD, directed by Mel Gibson (1995; Hollywood, CA: Paramount Pictures, 2002).

ABOUT THE AUTHOR

Les Parrott, PhD, is a *New York Times* number one bestselling author. He is cofounder, with his wife, Leslie, of the Center for Relationship Development on the campus of Seattle Pacific University. His books include *High-Maintenance Relationships*, *Love Talk* (with Dr. Leslie Parrott), *3 Seconds*, the award-winning *Saving Your Marriage before It Starts* (with Leslie), and the *New York Times* bestseller *The Hour That Matters Most* (with Leslie). Dr. Parrott is a sought-after speaker and holds relationship seminars across North America. He has been featured in *USA Today*, the *Wall Street Journal*, and the *New York Times*. His many television appearances include *The View*, *The O'Reilly Factor*, *CNN*, *Good Morning America*, and *The Oprah Show*. Les lives in Seattle with his wife and two sons. To learn more, please visit www.LesandLeslie.com.

Discover Your
Strength Profile

Your Strength Profile will help you find strength where you're not inclined to look by giving you

- a quick overview of where you currently stand on tapping into the power you can find in your head, heart, and soul;

- an in-depth look at the personal predispositions you are likely to have when it comes to the six most likely places to find strength; and

- several personalized exercises, selected for you based on your personal strength style.

Start living life with passion, meaning, and boldness *now*!

To take your online assessment, go to www.StrongerBook.com
and enter the coupon code STRONGER.

SMALL GROUP *INSIGHTS*

Where Real Relationships Start

Successful small group experiences depend on authentic relationships. The better the connections, the better the group. And that's just what this tool will do for you.

- Simple
- Personalized
- Engaging
- Quick

Whatever your group's purpose, the Small Group Insights Profile provides you with a fast-track to authenticity and meaningful connection.

www.smallgroupinsights.com

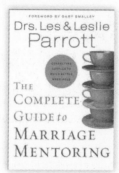

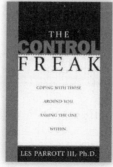